LOWSPEAK

LOWSPEAK

A DICTIONARY OF CRIMINAL AND SEXUAL SLANG

James Morton

ANGUS & ROBERTSON PUBLISHERS

16 Golden Square, London W1R 4BN,
United Kingdom and
United 4, Eden Park, 31 Waterloo Road,
North Ryde, NSW, Australia 2113.

First published in the United Kingdom by
Angus & Robertson (UK) in 1989

Text copyright © James Morton 1989

Typeset in Great Britain by Poole Typesetting (Wessex) Ltd., Bournemouth

Printed in Finland

British Library cataloguing in Publication Data
Morton, James
    Lowspeak: a dictionary of criminal and sexual slang.
    1. English language. Slang
    I. Title
    427'.9

ISBN 0 207 16229 8

For DOCK BATESON with love

Acknowledgements

I have listed in the bibliography the main reference works I have used as source material. Some are now out of print and even the publishers no longer have copies. I am therefore most grateful to those people who have lent me what are now, in both senses of the word, their valuable books. Even more I am indebted to those people who have provided me with words and their meanings. I list in no particular order Leonie Ferns, Brian Hilliard, Albert Prior, Laura Rosenberg, Esther and David Freedman who assisted with the Yiddish slang, Sheila Delaney, William Walter who contributed much of the naval slang, Peter Ewing for the army vocabulary, Fitzroy Drayton who did the same for black slang, Debbie Harman, Kim Egerton, if only for the troublesome jimscreeching, and many others. Particularly I have to thank all the police and those lawyers, probation officers, social workers, and others who when they came to Barnet Magistrates' Court, were plagued by me to provide contributions, and uncomplainingly did so.

Abbreviations

Aus	Australian
Bl	Black slang general
Can	Canadian
CRS	Cockney rhyming slang
Glas	Glaswegian
RS	Rhyming slang
SA	South African
Scots	Scots slang
SS	Street slang
UK	UK slang general
UKpol	UK police slang
US	US slang general
USbl	US black slang
USpol	US police slang
WI	West Indian slang
16c, 17c, 18c etc	16th century, 17th century etc

INTRODUCTION

In the early days of my criminal defence practice I had a client who spoke more or less in nothing but patois but never accepted that he did so. If you asked him what he had been doing before the police came or if indeed you read the statements made by him to the arresting officer of his denials of involvement in a particular crime it might go something like: 'I was having a pony down the carsi when the pikey schmo flashes me his groin and we're swagged by the filth down the peter over some smutter tom.'

He was most indignant when he saw this reduced to writing. He was an enormously fat man and would have wheezed up the stairs, plonked himself down, read through the statement and said 'Nice whistle you've got Mr M. Them apples aren't half hard on me plates. Gawd, what's this? It's a load of porkies. That copper's a right Hans Christian Andersen. You know I don't spiel like that.'

And so he genuinely believed. It was after another client of mine who, when asked to supply details of his alibi defence to a burglary replied, 'I was going case with a mystery' that I thought I should take closer order and discover just what they were talking about instead of having to say 'Pardon?' or 'Excuse me?' after every second sentence.

It seemed a sensible course of action particularly when I heard the following exchange at Horseferry Road Magistrates' Court. By 11 o'clock after a 10.30 start there was still no sign of the defendant. The police officer in the case leaned over to the man prosecuting to say, 'Chummy's legged it'. Seconds later the case was called and the young barrister rose to tell the magistrate, 'I'm afraid there'll be a delay in this case because, inexplicably, the defendant has chosen to walk to court.'

Working in London it was not difficult to get a rudimentary knowledge of criminal slang. There was, and still is for that matter, a good deal of hanging around outside courtrooms waiting for cases to be called. Defendants are all too happy to discuss something other than their case. It was either that or boxing, horse- or greyhound-racing. Much of the slang has passed into common speech helped on its way by programmes like 'Minder' and 'Eastenders' on television.

Rhyming slang (often known as Cockney Rhyming Slang, which is the most popular sort) is really just one example. Every city has its own rhyming slang said, like back slang, to have originally been a device to deceive the local police and provide a code. Until the other day I would have thought that anyone working in the criminal justice system would have had a fair knowledge of the basic vocabulary, but it is apparently not so. Judge Peter Mason, a barrister and judge of many years' standing wrote in *The Magistrate* (December 1988): 'I discovered the other day (though I'm told the phrases have been around for some time) that in certain quarters every prison sentence has its label . . .'

Since, as a rule of thumb, clients are more interested in how long they will get rather than whether they will be acquitted, he clearly did not spend much time chatting to his clients or he would soon have learned that a moon is a month, and so on. Either that or his clients were on their very best behaviour.

What is much more interesting, of course, is not that a moon is the word used for a sentence of a month but why it is. In that case it is self-explanatory and so are many others, but some terms defy explanation or have conflicting stories about their origin. 'Bill' or 'Old Bill' is one of the best examples of a phrase, the origins of which have become lost in folklore. In fact that one must be relatively new, but some go back to the seventeenth century and earlier.

Take 'angler' as an example. This was a common enough word for a man who used to steal from the open windows of houses by using a pole with a hook in Elizabethan times, and it was certainly in use after the Second World War. The detective Robert Fabian, one of the last glamour boys of Scotland Yard, wrote a number of books on crime and criminal behaviour and uses it as late as the 1970s. It has become almost obsolete in the last few years; people have now learned to shut their ground floor windows. But it lives on in another version. When I mentioned the word to a Kenyan friend of mine he replied, 'We call it pole fishing.'

Just as words and catchphrases find and then fade from favour, criminal and street slang changes almost monthly – even the crime can become obsolete. Just as 'angling' has gone, who ever heard of society women wearing stolen jewels as a sort of shop window for a fence nowadays. New words and phrases creep in and out of the language amazingly quickly. As part of the research for this book a friend of mine organised schoolchildren in North London to list words in common use; some used by the twelve-year-olds were regarded as passé by their friends a year older. Within days of the traitor Sir Anthony Blunt being exposed a client of mine came to see me about a case and explained that, 'I feel a right Sir Anthony'. Television and radio of course have a great deal to do with the popularisation of words.

Words have different meanings in different parts of the country let alone the world. 'Noncing' has almost always been the word used to describe child molestation in London but is apparently unknown in the North, whilst the word has been used to describe passing stolen cheques in Oxfordshire. It is not therefore suprising that words have such differing meanings in the UK and America. In England, for example, there would be nothing wrong with saying, 'I knocked my mother up this morning.' In the States it would be a criminal offence.

Except where the derivation seems obvious I have tried to give the meaning of the words and their derivation. It has not always been possible. Some words just defy all efforts to trace their origin. One such word was, I thought, 'jimscreech'. I first heard it from a friend in Willesden, used in the sense of obtaining entry to a flat by means of a con trick. None of the people I asked could think from where it derived and I thought for some time it was a word devised by a member of a team as a genuine attempt to provide a code. Then all became clear – or, relatively so – to 'jimmy' was to obtain free entry to a greyhound meeting. 'Jimscreeching' is simply a variant on that. It probably all goes back to the 'jimmy' or 'jemmy' the use of which obtained free entry to a house or safe.

It is highly likely that there will be other versions of how a particular word has come to be used in a context. Take 'Black Maria' as an example: one version I have given in this book is ingenious to say the least, the other was current in prison circles in the 1940s. I have no reason to suppose either is definitive and I shall be pleased to hear of other suggestions.

It may also be that some readers will violently disagree with the definitions. One of the problems with compiling a dictionary of this sort is that of triangulation, but I hope that in all but a handful of cases the words have been extant since the Second World War. I am all too conscious of a lecturer who gave a talk recently on current black street slang only to find that his students, from whom he had obtained much of the material, had happily invented the words for him. Nevertheless it may be that in ten years or so some of those words could actually be current.

James Morton,
1989

ABROAD; out and about and up to no good, particularly at night.

ACCIDENT; arrest, as in 'I had an accident' = 'I was caught.'

AC-DC; bisexual; derived from direct/alternate current.

ACE; 1. very good **2.** one dollar.

ACE, to; (US) to kill.

ACE IN THE HOLE;
something to give an advantage. In stud poker, which with five cards per player is perhaps the most interesting and best version of the game, the first card is dealt face down and is therefore seen only by the person to whom it is dealt. It is the 'hole' card and if an ace is of particular value. (In Cole Porter's song of the same name the advantage may come from the fact that 'some of them write to the old folks at home' (to send them money) 'whilst others have gals on that old tenderloin' – providing money for their lovers by prostitution to give them the necessary financial support.)

ACE OF SPADES; 1. a negro especially a very dark skinned one **2.** the female pudendum or vagina, from the shape and colour of pubic hair. An example of this is the old seaside postcard of a girl wearing black gloves and shoes saying she is going to a fancy dress party as the 'Five of Spades' **3.** a widow.

ACID; 1. lysergic acid **2.** cheek, as in 'Don't come the acid with me' **3.** officiousness.

ACROSS THE PAVEMENT; wages snatch.

ACTION, where's the;
'Where's the excitement?' but specifically **1.** where is there a card game or other form of gambling **2.** or where is a place

to meet women, even more specifically prostitutes or easy lays (qv).

AGAINST THE CLOCK; in a hurry.

AGGRO, a spot of; a problem to be solved or trouble to be overcome. 'To have had a spot of aggro' can often mean to have been arrested.

AIR DANCE; death by hanging.

ALADDIN'S CAVE; (UK) thief's hideaway for stolen goods.

ALIAS MAN; (WI) criminal, worthless person generally. Now almost exclusively black use, but originally 18c English.

ALL ON TOP; superficial, specifically to police evidence meaning the defendant has little fear of a conviction.

ALPHABET CITY; the avenues A,B,C,D,E around Manhattan's Lower East Side, a poor area.

ALPS, to go over the; to go to Dartmoor prison.

AMAMI NIGHT; more or less regular time for a cell search by prison officers. It came from the Shampoo advertisement, 'Friday Night is Amami Night.

AMBULANCE CHASER; a lawyer who attends scenes of accidents and hospitals to get business from the injured or bereaved who are not in a position to resist his blandishments.

ANCHOR; 1. stay of execution of death sentence **2.** a bribed juror who will be expected to vote for an acquittal and try to influence at least two others on the jury to obtain a hung jury.

ANCHOR, to swallow the; 1. to give oneself up to the police **2.** to give up crime, to retire.

ANDREW, or **ANDREW MILLER;** the navy. After the name of an extremely active pressganger during the Napoleonic Wars.

ANGEL; 1. someone supplying money to finance a

crime **2.** a sandwich board man **3.** a passive homosexual.

ANGELDUST; PCP, phencyclidine.

ANGLE, to; to scheme.

ANGLER; a thief who steals from ground floor open windows. The thief has a rod or pole, known as a curb, so that he can hook objects just inside the window. Dating from Elizabethan times, the term is now almost obsolete as fewer and fewer people living on the ground floor leave their windows open. The word was also used to mean pickpocket.

ANIMAL; 1. person without any moral code, a psychopath **2.** derogatory term used in gymnasia for a black boxer. 'All I got is animals in my stable (qv)' **3.** professional strongman on a gambling syndicate.

ARCTIC EXPLORER; a drug addict, from use of snow (qv).

ARM ON, to put the; to ask for a loan.

ARM, on the; eating and drinking without payment, principally by a police officer on the beat. It is a matter of considerable debate whether this is the first step to more serious corruption or is good policing in that by setting up a series of neighbourhood contacts the officer can hear what is happening on his patch. Those who think it leads to corruption point out that in return for the food the officer would be expected to overlook minor misdemeanours and perhaps be on hand to deal with troublemakers. In America and to a lesser extent in England a police officer will know of a number of restaurants and cafés where he can expect to have a certain number of free meals each year.

ARMY; person, often a tramp, with one arm or a crippled arm. See also *wingy*.

AROUND THE WORLD; service offered by prostitutes

which involves licking and sucking the client's body including the genitals and anus.

ARSE; the buttocks or posterior. Until about 1660 the word was used in standard English but from then on became mere slang.

ARSE BANDIT; homosexual.

ARSE-END; derogatory term, the dregs, the lowest as in 'Nigeria is the arse-end of the universe.'

ARSEHOLED; very drunk. Possibly because of the diarrhoea which would follow a heavy night's drinking.

ASH CASH; fee paid to doctor for signing cremation certificate.

ASHES HAULED, to have one's; to have sexual intercourse usually with a prostitute or stranger.

AT IT; 1. thieving either on a specific occasion or generally. As in 'What's he doing nowadays?' 'He's at it' **2.** having sexual intercourse. (A good example of a word or expression having both sexual and criminal connotations.)

AUNTIE; elderly male homosexual.

AWAY; to be in prison.

AWAY, to have it; 1. to have sexual intercourse **2.** to run off after a theft.

AWAY, to put it; to eat a great deal. A term of mock admiration as in, 'He can't half put it away.'

AXE; 1. knife **2.** razor **3.** guitar.

AXEMAN; prison barber.

AXLE GREASE; a bribe. The shortened version *axle* is more common.

B

B.A.B.; (pronounced bee-ay-bee) (US) bare ass beach, a nudist beach. On only a very limited number of beaches in the United States is nude bathing permitted.

BABBLER; (Aus) thief. Babbling brook = crook.

BABYLON; (WI 20c) **1.** The police, as in 'look out here comes Babylon.' From the belief amongst Rastafarians that the Biblical Babylon was a place of evil. In the Mandrake Club trial, following an affray in West London, much turned on the use of the word and whether it had been used as a signal to attack the police **2.** England **3.** white people generally.

BABYSITTER; (Can) prison officer.

BACK, at the; (UK 20c) drugs taken one after another.

BACK DOOR; (US 20c) anus. The English equivalent euphemism is back passage and has led to all sorts of music hall jokes about the efficacy of medicines taken in the parlour.

BACK DOOR MAN; 1. (USb1) a sodomite **2.** a married woman's lover, from the way he will leave by the back door when the husband enters the front.

BACK GATE DISCHARGE; 1. (US 19c) the death of a prisoner, ie the coffin goes out of the back gate of the prison **2.** (US) parole.

BACKING AND FILLING; the art of filling the mug (qv) with confidence prior to the con trick being worked on him.

BACKSTOP; a man who works directly behind the mark (qv). This was an expression particularly common in Chicago in the 1930s and used by older pickpockets. The true art of the pickpocket may well be becoming obsolete as it is replaced by steaming (qv).

BACKSTREET BUTCHER; an abortionist.
From the mess often made of the unfortunate girls on whom he has worked.

BACK UP; 1. (US) serial sex with a woman **2.** to distend the vein during drug taking **3.** (US) to allow the blood to come back into the glass during a vein shot **4.** (US) to refuse to make a connection (qv) on the fear that the addict might be a stool-pigeon (qv).

BAD; (USbl) very good. A reversal of values.

BAD COUNT; (US) **1.** an unfair decision as from boxing. The classic case of the bad count was in the Jack Dempsey-Gene Tunney fight when there was a famous long count of some 13 seconds allowing Tunney time to recover and later knock out Dempsey. In professional wrestling it is not uncommon to hear the referee count 'four – five – six – five – six' to enable a wrestler to regain his feet rather than have a bout end in an unscheduled way. **2.** a quantity of drugs that is smaller than that paid for.

BAD FALL; (US) an arrest

when the rapper (see *rap*) refuses to withdraw the charges. There seems to be no equivalent in UK of the word. The practice is, of course, common and the phrase is to 'get at', 'get into' or 'get to' the victim. Either threats or money will do the trick. The 'get to' presumably refers to the rare and serious case where the police have the victim or a witness is in hiding and guarded by the police.

BADGE; (US) policeman, from the badge worn.

BADGER-GAME; (US) a variation of a confidence trick. The victim goes to the hotel with a girl who is either very young or who looks it. Shortly before intercourse takes place but whilst the victim and girl are at least partially undressed the 'father' or 'uncle' of the girl bursts into the room and demands compensation for the violation of his 'under age' daughter. The compensation may in theory be to send her away to a school to forget about this experience. Occasionally, but more unusually, if an older girl is used, the 'father' role may become that of 'husband'.

BADMOUTH; (USbl) to disparage.

BAD SCENE; (US) a situation where trouble is likely to break out at any minute. Particularly used in the drug trade.

BAD TRIP; (US) an unpleasant experience whilst taking drugs, particularly LSD.

BAG; 1. (UK) a woman, almost invariably unattractive, and usually middle-aged or elderly. Although it does not seem to have been documented before the 1920s use probably goes back to the last decades of the 19c **2.** to catch as in 'bag a thief' from the game bag used in country sports **3.** (US) small packet of narcotics; either a dime bag (ten dollars) or a nickel bag (five dollars) Green (see bibliog.) points out that whilst the price remains the same the quantity diminishes as does its quality **4.** (US) scrotum **5.** condom **6.** (US) suppress **7.** (US 19c) an informer, obsolete since the

1930s **8.** (US) personal taste. Originally used in the drug trade but now in more common usage eg 'Drugs aren't my bag but drink is' **9.** (US) douche-bag used by prostitutes.

BAG, in the; 1. (US) drunk. From the habit of purchasing liquor from stores who put the bottles in a thick brown paper bag **2.** (UK) a certain success in the immediate future, possibly from when a poacher had the rabbit or other game 'in the bag' and unable to escape.

BAGGAGE; 1. (US) a watcher at a gambling table; a non-player; a kibbitzer (qv) **2.** women to be sent to Argentina as prostitutes.

BAGGAGE-BOX (or **-BOY**); (US) homosexual prostitute offering active as opposed to passive sex to clients; he will also offer fellatio.

BAGGED; 1. (UK) arrested **2.** (US) drunk.

BAGGER; a ring snatcher. The victim's hand is seized and the ring pulled off. From the French *bague* = a ring.

BAGGING; (UK) sexual intercourse. An expression used mainly in England's north country. An enquiry was made of the detecting ability of a Hull policeman: 'Well,' came the reply, 'it took him three years to find out someone was bagging his wife.'

BAGMAN; (US) a person who collects bribe money and delivers it to a judge or the police. The procedure is well documented in most reports into the behaviour of the New York police including the Knapp Commission report. This report into allegations of wholesale corruption was made in the early 1970s. Derided by the police as 'a tale concocted in a whorehouse' the testimony and tape recorded evidence was to prove overwhelming. There were similar revelations in other cities such as Philadelphia, Indianapolis and Chicago. See also *on the pad.*

BAGPIPE; (US) sexual intercourse where the penis is placed in the armpit; now almost exclusively homosexual. Like *huffle*, which means the same thing, has been extant since the18c. It has fallen into disuse in recent years, but has now been revived in homosexual usage.

BALD TYRE BANDIT; traffic policeman, from his checking on the roadworthiness of vehicles.

BALE; (US 20c) a pound or half kilo of marijuana.

BALL; 1. (US) sexual intercourse **2.** (UK) daily allowance of meat in prison. Probably obsolete since 1950s **3.** (US) a dollar; from a dollar bill or note easily crumpled in the hand; also a silver dollar.

BALL, to have a; to have a good time.

BALLBUSTER; 1. (US) something very difficult **2.** a women who deprives a man of his virility **3.** (US) a thief who grabs the victim by the testicles whilst his colleague takes the man's wallet. This is a variant on the clout and lam (qv) procedure.

BALL CRUSHER; a sexually active woman who exhausts a man. This differs from a ballbuster who will exhaust a man emotionally.

BALLOCKS WORKERS; (US) see *ballbuster 3.* Some writers wrongly think the word has been obsolete in England since the 19c. It is, however, now almost always spelled with an 'o'.

BALLOON; 1. (US) a small quantity of drugs wrapped in paper **2.** (RS) saloon. In New York under an old ordinance the word saloon could not be used on the fascia of the bar. Some owners got around this by calling them 'balloons'.

BALLS; 1. testicles **2.** nerve, as in 'He's got the balls to do it.' **3.** nonsense.

BALMY (often **BARMY**) **LANDING;** (UK early 20c) the prison landing which housed mentally disturbed prisoners.

BAMBER, to do a; to make a mistake. English police expression following an Essex case where some 20 police procedural blunders resulted in a multiple murder being thought to be suicide. The name derives from the murderer, Jeremy Bamber, who was sentenced to five terms of life imprisonment in 1986 for the murder of five members of his family in the hope of inheriting his adoptive parents' fortune. He had misled the police into believing that his sister Sheila had gone beserk with a shotgun, killed her family and then committed suicide. Bamber's appeal was dismissed in March 1988. Apparently, as with the American serial killer Ted Bundy, Bamber had received a quantity of 'fan mail' from female admirers.

BAM-POT; (Glas) a fool. Current in the 1960s which has now come to mean a dangerous and violent person of unstable mental condition.

BANANAS; 1. Special Patrol Group: 'they hang around in bunches and are yellow and bent' **2.** mad.

B and D; (US 20c) bondage and discipline.

BANDIT; generally derisory term used mainly by the police for a smalltime or unsuccessful thief, eg gas-meter bandit, a man who specialises in breaking open gas meters for the silver and coppers therein. See also *arse bandit*.

BANG; 1. (UK) to have sexual intercourse **2.** (US 19c) to steal a watch from a chain by breaking the holding ring with the thumb and forefinger. Now almost certainly obsolete **3.** (US) to steal a purse by twisting the clips **4.** (UK) injection of narcotics usually taken intravenously but now possibly subcutaneously **5.** the excitement from *4.* **6.** (US) to look at.

BANG A HANGER; to steal a purse.

BANGED UP; 1. (UK) locked up in a prison cell or particularly on remand, awaiting trial or sentence. The person

cannot get out and about and so the phrase may also mean **2.** pregnant **3.** suffering from VD.

BANG-UP; (US) excellent.

BANG TO RIGHTS; (UK 20c) East End phrase common from the 1930s. With no defence; *in flagrante delicto*. Used as follows 'I've got to plead. I'm caught bang to rights.' Originally meaning caught with stolen property, the phrase has become a traditional one because of police insistence in the 1950s and '60s that when arrested defendants would make this sort of admission. It went along with 'It's a fair cop, guv' and 'I only did it for the wife and kiddies.' These admissions were known as verbals (qv) and were invariably strongly and unsuccessfully challenged. Because of this the phrase is rarely heard in the criminal courts but often when the defendant speaks with his lawyer.

BARBS; barbiturates.

BAREBACK RIDER; (US and UK 20c) a man who has sexual intercourse without wearing a sheath. A common expression before the use of oral contraceptives.

BAR L; Barlinnie prison, Glasgow.

BARNDOOR; (UK) fly. 'The barn door's open' = 'Your fly is undone.'

BARNET; (CRS 1850) from Barnet Fair = hair. As in 'Keep your Barnet on.' A horsefair was held annually for 399 years in Barnet and abandoned in 1988.

BARNYARD PIMP; fried chicken, a staple dish in the American prison system.

BARON; 1. (US) a policeman assigned to a hotel beat **2.** (UK 20c) a dealer in tobacco in prison. This man can be the effective controller of the inmates. At the time of the disturbances at Parkhurst prison in the 1970s, the then baron had such control over the prisoners that no film show could begin until he had arrived to take his seat.

BASH; (UK) **1.** a smash and grab raid **2.** sexual intercourse **3.** prostitution. When prostitutes were, for a time, cleared from the streets following the Sexual Offences Act 1959 this meaning fell into disuse but is now enjoying a comeback, as are the prostitutes. Prostitution has never been a crime in English law. The offence is soliciting in public for immoral purposes.

BASH THE BISHOP, to; (UK 19c) masturbate. The uncircumcised penis resembles a bishop in a Staunton-designed chess set.

BASKET; 1. an illegitimate child **2.** male genitalia.

BASKET LUNCH; fellatio.

BASS; bastard. Glasgow dialect common from the 1960s onwards.

BATH, to take a; to lose a lot of money, especially after a trick. From the Yiddish *Er haut mikh gefirt in bod arayn* when, at the turn of the century, immigrants were tricked into taking off their clothes and going to a bathhouse for decontamination.

BAT PHONE; a policeman's personal radio. (From the strip cartoon character Batman who had a similar device).

BATTER, on the; (UK) **1.** an English north country expression for prostitution. A joke of the time was: 'There are two flies on a piece of Yorkshire pudding. Which one is the prostitute?' Answer: 'The one on the batter.' Green (see bibliog.) suggests this is now used of male prostitutes **2.** (Scots) going out drinking.

BATTY; (WI) the bottom or anus.

BATTYMAN; (WI) homosexual.

BATTY PAPER; (WI) lavatory paper.

BAY STATE; (US) a hypodermic needle, from the trade name.

BEAK; a magistrate or judge.

BEARD; a man, possibly but not necessarily, homosexual, used to squire the wife or girlfriend of a man unable to take her to previews, dinners etc.

The absentee husband may be either working away from home or in prison. The aim is to prevent her from becoming involved with other men.

BEARD, to don the; (Aus) cunnilingus.

BEAST; 1. (WI) a police officer **2.** a sex offender; the use is common amongst prisoners in Lancashire who do not know the term nonce (qv).

BEASTMAN; (WI) a policeman.

BEAT; a policeman's round.

BEAT, to; (US) **1.** to rob or mug **2.** to escape from prison.

BEAT THE RAP, to; to obtain an acquittal.

BEAVER; 1. a hat **2.** an ultra-smart salute made to a senior officer: 'Threw him up a right beaver, I did' **3.** the female pubic hair **4.** a beard. In the days when bearded men were less common a cry amongst children at the sight of one was 'beaver'.

BEAVER SHOT; the close-up view of the pubic hair obtained when a woman is not wearing pants.

BEEF, to; to complain.

BEESMAN; (WI) police.

BEGGAR'S LAGGING;
three-week prison sentence.
The standard sentence for
begging. Now in England and
Wales much to the fury of
metropolitan magistrates a
sentence of imprisonment cannot
be imposed for this crime. They
view the fiercer forms of begging
as being close to robbery.

**BEHIND THE EIGHT
BALL, to be;** to be in a
difficult position. From the pool
hall use of being behind the black
ball which must not be touched.

BEING ADRIFT; (Navy)
absent without leave; not at
one's place of duty.

BELL; the clitoris.

BELL, to give a; to
telephone.

BELLMAN; member of a
burglary team who specialises in
cutting off alarm systems.

BEND, to; 1. (US) to kill **2.**
(UK) to steal **3.** to distort, as in
evidence.

BEND BACKWARDS; to
persuade a witness or defendant
to change his mind yet again.
This occurs when a witness has
decided to give a statement
contrary to the one he gave the
police, now in the favour of the
defendant. The police, in taking
another statement, may bend
him backwards, pointing out the
undesirability from his (and their)
point of view of deviating from
his first statement. It can also
occur when an accused wishes to
change his solicitor for another
who is said to be able to get him
bail or a certain acquittal. Rather
than lose the client the first
solicitor will bend the client
backwards pointing out that he
really is the man for the job.

BENDER; 1. (RS) a
suspended prison sentence.
Bender = suspender **2.** a
sustained drinking bout.

BENNIES; Benzedrine
tablets.

BENT; 1. dishonest **2.** stolen
as in 'bent gear'.

BENT, to go; to inform or
turn Queen's Evidence. As in:
'Tom's gone bent on us.'

BERK; (CRS) a fool. Berkeley
Hunt = cunt. It is curious that
the name of no other hunt has
been used. It would be quite

easy to say 'He's a right Quorn', perhaps less to say 'He's a right Essex Farmer's.'

BERTIE SMALL; a police informer, a sneak. From the name of the first of the big supergrasses. In fact his name was Smalls and in the 1970s he informed on a considerable number of men with whom he had been involved in bank raids in the Wembley and north London area. In return he was given immunity from prosecution. This practice was condemned by the Court of Appeal who reduced some of the sentences on the men convicted by his evidence who had been given terms of imprisonment up to 21 years. He was the one and only supergrass to be given immunity. All his successors received prison sentences, albeit of a much reduced nature, which often meant their release when they had given the required evidence. In the meantime they were often kept in police stations with conjugal visits, colour television and regular outings to local public houses.

BERTIE, doing a; turning Queen's Evidence.

BEVVY; a drink.

BEVVYKEN; (SS) a public house or wine bar. *Bevvy* as a contraction of beverage has been current since the late 1970s, 'ken' is the 16c word for a house. By the middle of the 19c it had come to mean a small house or hotel frequented by criminals.

BEWER; a woman. Now not common but once used extensively by Irish tramps. Possibly from the Welsh *bodyer* = to feel.

BIBLE BASHER; a clergyman particularly an evangelist, from the pounding the bible receives from the preacher during a sermon.

BICE; 1. a two year prison sentence **2.** two pounds sterling. It derives from the French *bis* = twice.

BICYCLE; a sexually accommodating woman, not a prostitute. In his book *Owning Up*, George Melly refers to one such woman as the 'Widnes Bicycle'. One of Max Miller's sexually ambiguous songs was entitled 'I went for a ride on her bicycle'.

BICYCLE, on his; a boxer who 'pedals' backwards around the ring landing counter punches and hoping to tire his opponent is described in this way.

BIG C; 1. euphemism for cancer **2.** a caution in a minor case where no further proceedings are taken by the police.

BIG GATES; prison.

BIG HOUSE; prison.

BIG JOHN; a policeman, doubtless from the name of a particularly feared officer.

BIG ONE; £1000.

BIG ONE, to give it the; 1. to boast **2.** to intimidate.

BILL; 1. the police. It is difficult to obtain the correct derivation of the word. One version is that it comes from a policeman in the East End of London given to drink whose daughter was sent out at night to the local pubs to ask 'Is Bill here?' Another version is that it comes from the cartoon character by Bill Bairnsfeather. A third is that it refers to William IV, the reigning monarch when the Metropolitan Police was founded **2.** a taxi driver's licence.

BILL SHOP; a police station.

BIMBO; the girlfriend of a criminal; from the Italian *bambino*. In pre-war America the word was used for a young man. Now used for sexually active girl, possibly one who associates with older men.

BIN, the; 1. short for looney bin, a mental assylum **2.** a police or prison cell.

BIN, to; to lock up.

BINDLE; a roll of blankets or other possessions carried by a tramp.

BINDLE STIFF; a hobo or tramp.

BINGLE; (Aus) a traffic accident.

BINS; spectacles or binoculars, as used in 'Ref, you need bins.'

BINT; (Army) a woman particularly a young girl. From the Arabic *bint* = female camel.

BIRD; 1. a girl **2.** (CRS) a prison sentence. Birdlime = time (qv).

BIT; 1. a short prison sentence **2.** a girl as in 'I've got a bit on the side' **3.** sexual intercourse **4.** money as in 'The boat's (qv) got a bit put away.'

BITCH, the; (Can) indefinite prison sentence.

BIT OF A MESS; a prostitute's lover but neither her pimp nor a client.

BIZZIE; a police officer because he busies himself. See also *busy*.

BLACK, put the b. on; to blackmail.

BLACKBIRDING; the practice, after the abolition of slavery, of transporting Africans to America.

BLACK MARIA; the van which took prisoners to gaol. Originally the van was black and VR for Victoria Regina was painted on its side. 'Ria' was short for Victoria and the 'Ma' may have been mother. Or possibly named after a black Boston or New York boarding house keeper who was called on by the police if they could not cope with a particularly difficult drunk. A third version is that it was named after a black prostitute who was a regular guest of the van.

BLADE; a knife.

BLAG(GING); a robbery with violence. In use since the 1880s. A smash and grab raid (one where the window was smashed and jewellery stolen) was known as the blague. It may be a corruption of the French *bague* = a ring – something which was and is often stolen in a robbery or smash and grab raid.

BLANKET TREATMENT, to be given the; to receive a beating from prison officers.

BLAP UP, to; (UKbl) to deceive with fast talk.

BLAT; (US) a newspaper. From the German *blatter*, used by German-speaking immigrants.

BLEAT; 1. to inform to the police **2.** petition or appeal by a serving prisoner.

BLESSING; the arrival of an overdue monthly period. The opposite of curse.

BLIND PIG; an illegal drinking house.

BLINKY; a one eyed tramp. See also *wingy* and *army*.

BLISTER; a summons to appear in court.

BLITZ, to; to burgle or obtain entry to steal.

BLOCK; 1. the head, specifically the brain, as in 'Use your block' **2.** (Can) solitary confinement in prison.

BLOW; cannabis.

BLOW, to; 1. to leave a scene before the arrival of the police; to disappear **2.** to waste, as in spending money recklessly **3.** to fail to take an opportunity. As in golf: 'He blew a three-stroke lead going into the last.' **4.** to fellate.

BLOW A PETER, to; to open a safe with explosives.

BLOW AWAY, to; to kill by shooting.

BLOWER; 1. the telephone. **2.** The wire from a race-track to a betting office, which enables bookmakers to lay off bets which would result in too heavy a pay out. One of the great post-war racing coups was when a ringer (qv) was put in a race at Bath and the blower was cut to prevent the starting price of the winner being shortened by money coming through the offices on to the course when the SP (qv) would be determined.

BLOW JOB; fellatio.

BLOWN, to be; 1. to receive fellatio **2.** to have one's identity discovered.

BLUE-EYES; a wrestler designated to be the hero in a match, from 'blue-eyed boy'.

BLUEFLYER; a thief of lead from church roofs.

BLUE TAB; (Can) a trusty prisoner, from a band on his sleeve.

BLUEY; 1. lead, particularly from church roofs **2.** (Aus) a mate or friend, a term of endearment. Originally a red-headed man.

BOAT; 1. (RS) a face. Boat race = face **2.** an elderly person resident in a house to be burgled.

BOBBY; a police officer. Originally from Sir Robert Peel the founder of the Metropolitan Police. An article in *Police Review* in 1960 suggested that the term was now only used by tourists but it seems to have made something of a comeback and is in current use in the north of England.

BOFF, to; to have sexual intercourse.

BOGEY, or **BOGIE; 1.** a policeman **2.** nasal mucus. Also 'snot'.

BOILER; a woman of mature years who dresses in a young style. Probably from the fact that a middle-aged chicken must be boiled rather than roasted to be edible.

BOILERMAKER; 1. (US) a confidence trickster who has a way with women (particularly middle-aged) **2.** beer drunk with a whisky chaser.

BOMB; a large amount of money. In context: 'He made a bomb out of that one.'

BONK; to have sexual intercourse. There are a number of versions of the origin of this word, which probably dates back to the 1950s. One is the correlation between the head, also known as the bonk, and the penis, in the same way as (k)nob is used for either. 'He's got a bonk on' meant that a man or youth had an erection. *Bonkers* has for some time meant either mad or angry, and bonk is another instance of the association of violent crime and sex eg bang, screw, knock-off.

BOOB; 1. a fool **2.** police station **3.** prison. Short for *booby hatch* or *hutch*. By implication only fools would find themselves in one **4.** a breast.

BOODLE; from the Dutch *boedel*. Originally bad money but more generally stolen goods.

BOOST, to; originally the work of a shill (qv) in a gambling game who raised the excitement by pretending to play. More recently to shoplift. The shoplifter 'boosts' or lifts the article and then steals it.

BOOSTER DRAWERS; underwear worn by shoplifters in which to put the stolen goods.

BOOT, to put the b. in; to inflict severe, and often unnecessary, punishment. The phrase is used to describe a summing up adverse to the defence where the judge denigrates the defendant's witnesses. 'He didn't half put the boot in.'

BOOTNECK; a Royal Marine.

BOOTS; car tyres.

BORACIC; 1. a tall story, as in 'Don't come the boracic with me' **2.** (RS) impecunious. Boracic lint = skint.

BOTTLE AND STOPPER; (American west coast RS) a policeman. Bottle and stopper = copper.

BOTTLE OF SKINS; two elderly ladies, often sisters and spinsters who have lived together all their lives. This is a good example of words being used by criminals as a code. The phrase was coined by a team of house-breakers in the late 1970s in and around Darlington but has since passed into more general use in the north of England.

BOTTLE, on the; 1. to be an alcoholic **2.** (UKbl) a pickpocket. The phrase has been in use for over 50 years and is now used principally by black pickpockets on the underground.

BOTTLE, to lose one's; (CRS) to lose one's nerve. Bottle and Glass = arse. Literally the person has fouled himself through fear.

BOTTLER; 1. (UK) a person who collects money for a busker. A bottle was used in preference to a bag or hat in order to prevent spectators from removing the takings **2.** (US) a girl who works in a brothel where drinks are sold.

BOW, on the; short form of *on the elbow*. Scrounging.

BOW AND ARROW; (Can) position where a prisoner is handcuffed with his hands behind his back and his ankles and hands joined.

BOX; 1. a safe **2.** the vagina **3.** prison cell. Something which has to be opened **4.** a guitar.

BOXHEAD;(Army) a German.

BRAINS, the; the CID.

BRASCO; (Aus) an outside lavatory.

BRASS; a prostitute, from brass nail = tail. No longer commonly used in Britain, tail dates back to mid-Victorian times as a word for prostitute. In US it denotes sexual behaviour: 'Did you get any tail last night?'

BRASS MONKEY WEATHER; an extremely cold spell. From the saying 'It's cold enough to freeze the balls off a brass monkey.'

BREAD; money. Not American as might be supposed, but from rhyming slang. Bread and honey = money.

BREK; the last meal for a prisoner before his release. A few days before his release a con (qv) will be able to say 'Only four-three-two and a brek to go.' See also *porridge*. On the eve of his release both the prison officer and the convict will speak of the latter having time only for a 'Shit, shave and shampoo.' A naval version of this expression is the alliterative 'Short sharp shit shave and shampoo ready for shore leave.'

BREW; illicit alcohol in prison.

BREWER'S DROOP; the inability to get an erection caused by an excess of beer. Less common but with the same meaning is 'vintner's droop'.

BRIDEWELL; 1. police cells **2.** (Liverpool) the charging officer.

BRIEF; 1. lawyer, particularly a barrister. From the instructions sent to him **2.** a driving licence **3.** a letter **4.** a cheque **5.** a search warrant.

BRISTOLS, a pair of; (RS) the breasts. Bristol City = titty.

BROAD; 1. (US) a woman **2.** (UK) a playing card **3.** (UK) a credit card.

BROADSMAN; a cardsharper, three card trickster.

BRONZE; faeces. From the colour.

BROWN BREAD; (RS) = dead.

BROWN HATTER; male, often rich, homosexual.

BROWN NOSE, to; to curry favour; an even less polite version of 'arse licking'.

BUBBLE; (RS) **1.** to inform to the police. From bubble and squeak. **2.** a Greek, from the same rhyming slang.

BUCK; (Liverpool) young upwardly mobile criminal probably aged between 17 and 25.

BUCKESS; female young upwardly mobile criminal.

BUCKET; (Can) gaol.

BUGGER, to; to engage in anal intercourse. The term derives from a group of Bulgarian heretics in the Middle Ages who were falsely accused of indulging in sodomy.

BULL; 1. a police officer. Originally from America and used in the 19c, now in use in England amongst young West Indians **2.** (Can) prison guard.

BULLERMAN; (WI) police officer.

BUM, to; to borrow, particularly with no intention of repaying the lender, as in 'Can I bum a fag off you?'

BUM BANDIT; a homosexual, particularly one

who will openly solicit other males in steam baths, saunas and bars.

BUM BAY, to drop anchor in; to have anal intercourse.

BUM FLUFF; 1. soft lavatory paper. Until the 1950s this type of paper was not generally available and early versions tended to disintegrate during use **2.** the down grown on a young man's face at puberty.

BUM FUCK; anal intercourse.

BUMMER; 1. an unpleasant or boring experience **2.** a homosexual.

BUNG; a bribe.

BUNK-UP; sexual intercourse.

BUNNY; the victim of a confidence trick.

BUNNY, to; to talk indiscriminately. From 'to rabbit on' (qv).

BURGLAR BRIGADE; officers in prison service who inspect the anus of a prisoner for concealed drugs.

BURIED, to be; to have a bad fall at steeplechasing.

BURN; prison tobacco. This is roll-your-own as opposed to the more highly prized tailormade. Far more commonly used than snout (qv).

BURN, to; 1. to die by electrocution **2.** to cheat **3.** to kill, specifically by shooting.

BURNT; 1. (RS) window. Burnt cinder = window. **2.** to have contracted venereal disease.

BURY, to; to sentence to a term of imprisonment.

BUSH; the female pubic hair.

BUSINESS GIRL; euphemism for a prostitute.

BUSK, to; to pretend or improvise.

BUST, to; to raid, to arrest.

BUSTLE PINCHING, or **PUNCHING;** the male practice of rubbing up against women in crowded places such as the underground for sexual excitement. The correct word is frottage.

BUSY; a detective.

BUTT FUCK; anal intercourse.

BUY, to; to accept a story, particularly an untrue one. As used in 'I just hope he'll buy it.'

BUYER; a receiver of stolen goods who will buy them at a price far below their worth. Although a defendant will always prefer to plead guilty to receiving stolen property rather than the theft itself the sentence he may receive is not always that different in practice, particularly if it appears the receiver is a professional one. A common remark passed by judges whilst sentencing defendants in such cases is 'If there were no receivers there would be no thieves.'

BUY THE FARM, to; 1. to die. An extension of the Second World War phrase 'He bought it'. To buy a farm was a traditional hope of the city worker on his retirement **2.** to make a terrible mistake, as presumably it is to die. It is possible that in this context the phrase derives from baseball. In America there are farm clubs in the minor leagues to which major league players who have lost their form or have in some way misbehaved are sent for rehabilitation.

BUZZ; 1. pleasurable sensation obtained from taking drugs **2.** rumour: 'There's a buzz going round.'

BUZZ, to; to pick someone's pocket. Now extant only in the East End of London.

C; cocaine.

CACKLEBERRY; an egg. Originally tramps' slang, it now has wider usage particularly in Scotland. Cackler was a synonym for a hen in 17c literature.

CAD; 1. a rotter or low person. The word was at one time a warning meaning: 'constable in disguise' **2.** (US) a ration of drugs. An abbreviation of Cadillac (qv).

CADILLAC; an ounce of heroin or, less usually, cocaine.

CAGE; prison.

CALENDAR; one year's imprisonment.

CAN; 1. prison **2.** lavatory **3.** a safe (all need to be opened) **4.** buttocks.

CANARY; a police informer.

CANARY, to sing like a; to confess to a crime, often implicating others.

CANDY; heroin.

CANDYMAN; drug dealer trafficking specifically in heroin.

CANDLE; (RS) a ponce. Candlesconce = ponce.

CANE, to; to smash or beat up. Often used in relation to stealing from cars by smashing the quarterlight, as in 'I caned it with a stone.' It can also apply to tearing out car radios: 'I tried to cane the speakers.' Although now in current use it had been dormant since the 1920s.

CAP; 1. narcotics in capsule form **2.** oral sex.

CAPER; a crime of any sort.

CARD; to have your card marked; to be given inside information about, for example, the possibility of a police raid, or the availability of stolen goods. At a race meeting there used to be a number of tipsters outside the track who would pretend to have inside information from a particular stable about the prospects of a particular horse. In return for a few shillings they would 'mark your card' by circling the number of the horse supposed to win. In addition to the tipsters payment a lesser sum was added 'for the stable lad, sir' who had in theory provided the tout with the information in the first place.

CARD, to go through the; to back (or tip) all the winners at a horse or greyhound meeting.

CARNIVAL; sexual position where the woman sits on the man's face. From 'Do you know how to play carnival?', Answer: 'Yes I sit on your face and you guess my weight'. Guessing the weight competitions were a common fairground attraction. If the weight was guessed incorrectly the punter went to the scales free.

CARPET; 1. three months' imprisonment. It is said it took 90 days to weave a carpet on a prison loom. Another version is that it is rhyming slang: carpet bag = drag. *Dragging* was also the term for stealing from motor vehicles and a common sentence

for this or being a 'suspected person loitering with intent to commit a felony' was three months. **2.** three pounds.

CARPEY; to be locked in a prison cell for the night. From Latin *carpe diem*.

CARRY THE TORCH, to; to love unrequitedly. This probably arose from the feelings of a prostitute for her pimp. One of the standard ways of recruitment is for the man to pretend to be the devoted lover of the girl and then gradually to ease her into prostitution by persuading her into bed with 'a friend' on 'just one occasion' to help with the rent.

CARSI; lavatory. There is considerable dispute whether

this word comes from the Italian *casa* meaning house or from the Arabic. The long-held opinion is that it comes from the Italian.

CASE, to; to watch 2. to look over a location prior to a robbery or burglary.

CASE GOING, to have a; to be sleeping with a girl.

CASEKEEPER; brothel keeper.

CASE, on the; earning as a prostitute from only one client.

CASH IN ONE'S CHIPS; to die. PG Wodehouse's attractive variation was 'to hand in one's dinner pail'. (In America – where Wodehouse lived for much of his life – secretaries, factory workers, labourers would take their lunch to work in a little pail.)

CAT; 1. a thief with an iron nerve, as in *cat burglar*. The implication is that he is as cold-blooded and as agile as a cat **2.** the cat o'nine tails. See also *pussy* **3.** a young homosexual

man, abbreviation of catamite.

CATCH A COLD; to lose a considerable sum of money through gambling.

CATCHING PIGEONS; description of a horse working extremely well on the home gallops in training.

CATHOUSE; a brothel. Probably from the enthusiasm of tomcats for sexual intercourse.

CATTED, to be; to be allocated in prison to Category A. This denotes a prisoner who is a potential escapee and a danger to the public if he does so. In an English prison the potential escapee will be put in *patches* ie coveralls with luminous yellow patches on the trousers.

CAUGHT, to get; an unwelcome pregnancy.

CHAIR; the electric chair.

CHANCRE MECHANIC; (pronounced shangker) ship's doctor or his assistant. From the incidence of veneral disease amongst sailors.

CHANNEL FEVER; the impatience to reach port after a long voyage, coupled with the realisation that there is the prospect of having sex.

CHANNEL FEVER PILLS; apocryphal white or green jelly beans brought home by a sailor to be thrown on the lawn, white jelly beans for winter and green for summer. Aim was to keep the children busy in garden searching for the sweets whilst intercourse took place inside.

CHAPPER; (Yiddish) a policeman.

CHARLIE; 1. cocaine **2.** (Aus) a prostitute.

CHARLIE WOOD; see *Wood, Charlie.*

CHARVER, to; to have sexual intercourse. Originally a theatrical expression meaning an embrace, the word had become almost obsolete but now seems to be making a comeback.

CHASE THE DRAGON, to; to sniff heroin.

CHAVERED; tired out, possibly from too much charvering?

CHAW, to; to arrest, particularly pickpockets on the underground.

CHAWRY GOODS; stolen property.

CHERRIES; (RS) dogs = cherryhogs, specifically greyhounds. Used as in 'I won a monkey (qv) on the cherries.'

CHERRY; 1. a virgin **2.** any inexperienced person eg an apprentice jockey **3.** to blush.

CHEW THE FAT or **RAG;** to discuss and reminisce.

CHIB; a knife.

CHICAGO PIANO; tommy-gun used in the Chicago gang wars of the 1920s. The weapon, which fired up to 1000 .45 cartridges a minute, originally cost less than $200.

CHICKEN; a young boy, often truanting from school or home, on his own in London and prey to homosexual overtures.

CHICKEN, to be; to be cowardly.

CHICKEN HAWK or **HUNTER;** homosexual who seeks out under age boys.

CHICKEN RANCH;
generically a brothel. Referred
originally to a brothel in La
Grange, Texas, which was in
existence for nearly 130 years
until it was closed in 1973.

CHICKEN SCRATCH; the
practice of a drug addict crawling
around on the floor to find specks
of drugs, particularly crack.

CHILDREN; (RS) house-
breaking instruments. Boys and
girls = twirls, ie skeleton keys
(qv).

CHILL, to; to kill.

CHIP, to; carry out petty
crimes.

CHIPPIE; 1. a young girl, not
necessarily but sometimes a
prostitute. From the verb *to
chippy*, to have intercourse **2.** a
mark (qv).

CHIPPING; a version of the
corner game (qv). The girl
pretends to be a prostitute and
then disappears with the cash
before any sex can take place.

CHIV; a cut throat razor,
sometimes a knife or other
weapon for cutting or stabbing.
In 18c England 'to chive' meant
'to cut off', but 'chiv' meaning
knife *per se* seems to have come
from America at the end of the
18c. Chivs were often home-
made from a sharpened file or
screwdriver. *Chiving*, apart from
meaning to slash with a razor,
was the particular term for
pushing a broken glass into a
victim's face. It was particularly
common on race-tracks in the
1930s when pitched battles were
fought between rival gangs over
who should control the
bookmaking at the track.
Chiving, as a term rather than as
a practice, has now more or less
disappeared and the more
prosaic *glassing* has replaced it.

**CHOCOLATE
FREEWAY;** the anus.

CHOIRBOYS; (US) rookie, ie
newly recruited policemen.

CHOIR PRACTICE; an
informal meeting of police
officers.

CHOKED, to be; to be annoyed, upset, as in 'I wasn't half choked when I got that pull (qv).'

CHOKEY; prison, often solitary confinement. From the Hindustani *chauki* = gaol.

CHOPPER; 1. a helicopter **2.** a machine gun **3.** the penis **4.** a bicycle.

CHOPPERS; 1. the teeth **2.** the plural of *chopper* above.

CHOW; food. From to chew or to chaw a piece of tobacco.

CHRISTER; evangelist, often born again, and often one in charge of food distribution or a mission where religion is part of the diet.

CHUBB, to; to lock. From the name of the locksmith.

CHUCKED, to be; 1. to be acquitted **2.** to be rejected by ones lover.

CHUMMY; anyone of whom a policeman is speaking but usually a suspect, as in '. . . and then chummy does a runner'.

CIRCUS; a sex show.

CIVILIAN; someone who is neither a police officer nor a working criminal.

CLARET; blood. A boxing term as in 'The claret flowed in round two.' Particularly common in south London not necessarily in connection with boxing.

CLEAN; 1. free from drugs or stolen property when searched by the police **2.** someone without criminal convictions.

CLEAN WHEELS; a motor vehicle to be used in connection with a crime which has not previously come to the notice of the police.

CLIMBER; a burglar who literally climbs up the outside of buildings, particularly hotels. There is now said to be only one working in London.

CLINK; prison. From the old gaol in Clink Street, Southwark, London.

CLINKERS; (Aus) pellets of faeces sticking to anal hair. Originally 19c English.

CLIP, to; to cheat, not necessarily for a very large amount of money and refers specifically to a prostitute who works a version of the corner game (qv) taking money and telling the client to go to a room and wait for her.

CLIPJOINT; low drinking club, dancehall or bar, where the victim will be clipped ie lead in to buying a hostess champagne which is in reality only lemonade. It is not necessarily the case that sexual services will be available but it is certainly the intention of the management that the visitor should think this is so.

CLOCK; the face.

CLOCK, to; 1. to time, as in horse racing: 'I clocked him over five furlongs' **2.** to watch **3.** to recognise **4.** to hit **5.** to count money.

CLOTHESLINE; move in professional wrestling where when one man comes off the ropes at speed and is seemingly hit in the throat by the other with his forearms held at right angles to the body. In rugby football this is known as a straight arm

tackle, and is punishable by a penalty or by sending the offender off.

CLOTHESLINER; derogatory term for a petty criminal, not necessarily one who steals from clotheslines.

CLOUT; 1. influence **2.** the vagina.

CLOUT, to; 1. to hit **2.** to steal. The word is still common amongst north London school children.

CLOUT AND LAM; literally to steal and run. In the 18c clouts were pocket handkerchiefs and there was a ready market for stolen ones. *Clouting* came to mean stealing these handkerchiefs but the meaning was widened to cover all pickpocketing. To lam is to run away. See also *on the lam*.

CLUB NUMBER; the criminal record number of a person convicted of previous offences. On subsequent arrest the details of the suspect's last three offences are passed to the Crown Prosecution Service, eventually to be read in court.

CLUDGIE; (Scots) an outside lavatory, often an earth closet.

COAT; a suspect, as in 'Have you got a coat?'

COAT, to; to tell off, or to scold, as in 'I gave him a right coating.'

COBBLERS; (CRS) **1.** testicles. Cobbler's awls = balls **2.** money: 'I done me cobblers' = 'I've lost all my money' **3.** rubbish, as in 'It's a load of cobblers.'

COCK; 1. the penis **2.** a person, often a publican or scrap metal dealer, invited by an officer to a police function in the certain knowledge that the cock will pay for the evening's entertainment. The cock also knows this and will expect certain favours in return. Possibly it comes from the rhyming slang: cock and hen = ten. The cost, in years gone by, of such an evening out.

COCK A DEAF 'UN; to refuse to listen as in 'The ref cocked a deaf 'un to the fancy and gave it to the home boy.'

COCK AND HEN; 1. (RS) a sentence of ten years' imprisonment. See also *cock*. **2.** ten pounds.

COCK SUCKER; originally the female partner in a male homosexual relationship but now in general use a derogatory term.

COCK TEASER; a young girl who will lead a man on and then refuse to have full sexual intercourse.

COCONUT; term of racial abuse amongst West Indians, suggesting pro-white feelings – brown outside, white inside.

CODIE; a child molester. Possibly it originated from a molester of that or a similar name. See also *short eyes* and *nonce*.

COFFIN NAIL; a cigarette, from the suggestion that it induces cancer.

COLD TURKEY; a hard way of coming off a drug addiction. It is done by not taking any tranquillising or substitute drugs such as methadone. One of the side effects is the way the skin becomes pimpled like turkey or goose skin.

COLLAR, against the; something done the hard way; an uphill finish on a race.

COLLAR; a policeman.

COLLAR, to; to arrest.

COLLAR, to have one's c. felt; to be arrested.

COLLAR AND TIE BRIGADE; lesbians.

COLLEGE; prison, more specifically Borstal. As in 'He's just come out of college.'

COME; semen or the female viscous fluid produced in climax.

COME ONE'S COCOA; 1. to ejaculate **2.** (UK) to confess to the police.

COME, to; to ejaculate.

CON; 1. a prisoner, a shortened form of convict **2.** a trick, shortened form of confidence trick.

CON, to; to cheat or swindle.

CONFUSION; (WI) a street fight.

CONK; 1. the head and, now more usually **2.** the nose.

CONNECTION; 1. an arrangement with a supplier of drugs **2.** the relationship of a minor criminal to a major one. This will provide him with protection against predations of other criminals and to a certain extent against the police.

CONS; the previous convictions (criminal not religious) of an accused.

COON; derogatory term originally for a negro but now used for all black people. A diminutive of racoon which southern negros were supposed to enjoy eating.

COOPING; the practice of uniform police sleeping on duty. It is also known as *holing* or *huddling*.

COP, to; 1. to arrest **2.** to receive something generally unpleasant as in 'I copped a blister,' = 'I received a summons' **3.** to accept a bribe as in 'Will he cop?' = 'Will he accept a bribe?'

COP, to be on the; to be about to have an orgasm.

COP A LIE or **LIEDOWN;** to be sentenced to a term of imprisonment.

COP AND BLOW, to; to exploit a prostitute.

COP A PLEA, to; to plead guilty in the hope of a lighter sentence.

COPPED HIS LOT or **LOAD;** to have ejaculated prematurely.

COPPER'S NARK; a regular police informer.

CORN; money as in *serious corn* meaning a lot of money. Originally from the ease with which corn could be used as currency. Mainly black slang nowadays. A variation is in horse racing, when at the end of the season the horses are said to run in the *Haycorn Stakes*, hoping to earn enough for their winter keep.

CORNER; a share in proceeds of crime.

CORNER GAME; a confidence trick in which, in its simplest form, the mark (qv) buys what he believes to be high quality goods at a low price. They are in fact shoddy items. This works particularly well with perfume sold out of suitcases. Another example is when the punter pays his money and is told to wait around a corner or up some stairs, after which he will be taken to see a blue movie while the tricksters run off in the opposite direction. A more sophisticated version is to have the mark buy 'stolen goods' and then to be arrested by fake policemen. He may then be able to bribe them to obtain his release. In any version he loses most if not all his money.

CORNHOLE, to; to commit the act of buggery, often forcibly.

COSH, to; to hit with weighted object. From Romany *koshter* = a stick.

COSH, to be under the; to be in someone's power, to do their bidding.

COTTAGE; homosexual meeting place, usually a public lavatory.

COTTAGING; the practice of frequenting public lavatories in the hope of casual sex.

COUGH, to; to confess as in 'He wouldn't cough even if he had bronchitis.'

COUNTING RIVETS; (Navy) going to sleep. Refers to lying down and looking at the rivets above the bunk.

COUNTRY, the; Dartmoor prison.

COW; 1. Glaswegian word for a promiscuous girl who will perform with a line-up of boys. This possibly explains the reluctance of some women in the 1960s to use the word when citing examples of their husband's foul language in support of a divorce petition. They preferred the euphemism 'meadow lady' **2,** (RS) a wife. Cow and kisses = missus.

COZZER; policeman. Amalgamation of copper and rozzer.

CRABS; Naval and army slang for the RAF. One version of the origin is that the uniform is the same colour as the ointment once used to remove crab lice from the pubic hair. A second is that when the RAF first paraded in uniform an admiral, on seeing them, remarked they resembled the line of fat under the shell of a crab.

CRACK; 1. cocaine baked into crystals with baking powder and ammonia. It is smoked and produces a fast high. It is also highly addictive **2.** the vagina **3.** a joke, a bit of fun.

CRACKLING; a sexually appetising woman, as in 'A nice piece of crackling'.

CRAP; 1. to defecate. See also *crapper* **2.** rubbish, as in 'That's load of crap.' It may be either words or inferior quality goods which are said to be crap.

CRAPPER; a lavatory. Named after Thomas Crapper, the Yorkshireman who is credited with the invention of the modern flushing lavatory. It is another example of the name of the inventor, or organiser being given to the product as in Hooker (qv). It is said that a primitive version of the water closet was invented in Elizabethan times, but that when the design was shown to the Monarch the inventor had drawn carp or goldfish swimming in the water. This did not appeal and the design came to nothing.

CRASH; 1. to sleep **2.** to write off an offence, eg a domestic assault thought to be more trouble than its worth. Also known as *cuffing*.

CRASH PAD; a place solely for sleeping in.

CREAM, to; 1. to kill or wipe out **2.** to have an unexpected orgasm **3.** to steal from an employer or partner.

CREEPER; a hotel or house burglar. An alternative, but similar meaning is a thief working in collaboration with a prostitute. Whilst the prostitute entertains the client the creeper enters the rooms and empties the man's pockets.

CREEPING AND TILLING; (UBbl) stealing from shop tills.

CREW; a gang of boys who work together as a unit in secret crime.

CRIB; a safe.

CRO; Criminal Record Office but used for the form 609 supplied to the courts setting out the details of the defendant's previous convictions. Traditionally in magistrates' courts only the last three are read out by the prosecution unless they are specifically asked to do otherwise by the court.

CROAK, to; to die.

CROAKER; 1. a professional killer and therefore **2.** a doctor, specifically a prison doctor **3.** a police informer, one who will turn QE (qv).

CROMO; (Aus) prostitute.

CROW; a look out man in a three-card trick team.

CRUCIAL; (WI) a multi-purpose word meaning both necessary and fashionable. 'That's a crucial suit,' and 'Dangerously crucial' are used to mean exceedingly fashionable, necessary.

CRUD; 1. originally referred to dried semen which clings to the body or clothing but now more generally used as 2. any skin infection 3. syphillis 4. rubbish, as in 'It's a load of crud.'

CRUDE; an informer's tip off to the police as opposed to one given by a member of the public.

CRUMPET; a woman viewed in wholly sexual terms.

CRUSHER; a policeman, diminutive of beetle crusher from the way his feet would crush an insect.

CUFF, on the; refers to goods obtained on credit.

CUSHTI; an exclamation of approval, as in 'Your case is adjourned until after Christmas.' 'Oh cushti!'

CUT; 1. a share of profits 2. the mixing of a drug, eg heroin, with powdered sugar to increase the profits.

CUT THE MUSTARD, to; 1. to come up to standard 2. to get an erection. Mostly used in the negative: 'He can't cut the mustard any more'.

CUT THROAT DEFENCE; the situation in a criminal case where two or more defendants will try to lay the blame on each other. The result is often that all are convicted.

CUT UP TOUCHES, to; to reminisce (often in prison) over past crimes.

D

DABS; Fingerprints. A dab was originally a high-class rogue. The term lasted for 300 years or so but died out in the 19c. The use of dabs for fingerprints is, of course, fairly recent since fingerprinting as an exact science became known only at the turn of this century.

DADDY; 1. a male lover, often elderly, who supports a woman in return for sexual favours. Usually called *sugar daddy* (qv) **2.** prison baron, sometimes called *big daddy*.

DAGGA; South African term for cannabis.

DAISY-CHAIN; several persons having sexual intercourse simultaneously, group intercourse.

DANCE, to; to steal from upper floors of buildings. In the 17c the dance was a staircase, and the use of the word to mean stealing is originally 19c.

DANCE FLOOR; condemned cell, from the continual pacing of the prisoner.

DARBIES (also **DARBEYS** and **DARBYS**); **1.** handcuffs. The use is very old and originally included fetters **2.** the iron clad terms of a money lender.

DASH; originally a gratuity but now a bribe.

DC; standing for detention centre. Formerly a place for young offenders serving a short sentence.

DEAD RINGER; a person, horse or dog who is almost identical to another, and, in the case of a person, ideal for an identification parade. In the case of a horse or greyhound it can be substituted for another in a race for betting purposes. One of the last known examples was Flockton Grey which ran in a race for two-year-old horses at Stockton when it was three. Unsurprisingly it won easily, because of its extra strength.

DEAD SOLDIER; an empty bottle. Variations include *dead man*, *dead marine*.

DEAL; a plea bargain where under an arrangement between prosecution, judge and defence the defendant receives a shorter or even non-custodial sentence in return for a plea of guilty. If he had contested the case and been convicted, the defendant's punishment would have been harsher.

DEAL, to; 1. to trade in narcotics **2.** (SA) to cheat, as in 'Did they deal you then?'

DEANER or **DEENER; 1.** a shilling. Originally a racing expression **2.** a miser, ie someone who hoards deaners.

DEAR JOHN; letter sent to a prisoner or soldier serving overseas, by a wife or girlfriend terminating a relationship. Traditionally it begins 'Dear John, I have met this man and am having his baby . . .'

DECK; small packet of narcotics.

DECK, COLD; pack of cards which, unbeknown to the victim, has been pre-dealt.

DECK, to; to knock down.

DECKO or **DEKKO;** (from Urdu) a look, as in 'Have a decko out the window.'

DEEP SEA FISHERMAN; cardsharp on an ocean-going vessel.

DEEP SIX, to; to kill. From the naval term of throwing unwanted items overboard where they would drop to six fathoms.

DEPS; depositions in criminal cases taken at the magistrates' court to see whether the prosecution can establish a *prima facie* case against the defendant before he is committed for trial before a judge and jury.

DEUCE; a two-year prison sentence.

DIAMOND; 1. term of approval, as in 'You're a diamond' **2.** East End Jewish prostitute from Koh-i-Noor = Cohen whore.

DIBBLE; police officer. From the character in the children's cartoon film *Top Cat*.

DICK(S); 1. police. As far back as Elizabethan times Dick was the name given to a simpleton **2.** head or body lice **3.** (RS) the penis. Dickory dock = cock.

DICKLESS TRACEY; (Aus) policewoman or traffic warden. Derived from US cartoon strip *Dick Tracy*.

DIDDIKOI; gypsy (strictly a half-bred Romany).

DIDDLER; (Can) sex offender.

DIDO; an internal police complaint, ie not made by a member of the public.

DIG; 1. to punch, as in 'I gave him a dig in the kisser' **2.** to understand, as in 'Do you dig it?'

DIGGER; 1. (Can) punishment cell **2.** (Army) a table knife.

DIHEDRAL; (RAF) degree of dishonesty in a prison officer. Used in this context: 'What's his dihedral?'

DIKE, or **DYKE;** originally a woman with strong masculine traits but now almost exclusively used to mean lesbian.

DILBERRIES; (US) faeces which cling to the hair of the anus. See also *fartleberries*.

DILDO; 1. a false penis often used in a lesbian relationships **2.** an incompetent, from the fact that the sex aid is incapable of independent action.

DINAH; nitro-glycerine.

DIP; pickpocket.

DIPPED IN, or **OUT, to be;** to have good luck (or bad).

DIPPING AND PEERING; the act of soliciting men in cars.

DIP SQUAD; team of police designed to eliminate pickpocketing on the underground, at racecourses etc.

DIRT; prison term for sugar.

DIRT BOX; the anus.

DIRT BOX, up the; anal intercourse.

DISH OUT THE PORRIDGE; hand out prison sentences.

DISS, to; (WI) to disparage. 'He dissed me so I striped (qv) him'.

DISTRESS, to; (UKbl) to carry out mass robbery, particularly on the underground, where up to 30 thieves will take over a carriage or train and systematically rob the passengers.

DIVE; a low drinking house.

DIVE, to take a; to lose a boxing contest deliberately, *go in the tank* (qv). This can be done either for betting purposes or to build up the reputation of a local boy.

DIVER; pickpocket.

DIVOT; a toupee

DO, to; 1. to kill **2.** to beat up badly **3.** to commit a theft **4.** to search (especially of the police) **5.** to swindle or cheat.

D.O.A.; dead on arrival (at hospital). The body is often sent straight to the morgue, thereby avoiding complicated paperwork.

DO A DRUM, to; to commit an act of house-breaking.

DO A LIVIN', to; to commit a one-on-one robbery.

DO A RUNNER, to; 1. to escape from the police **2.** to abscond bail.

DOG; 1. unattractive woman **2.** general term of abuse as in 'That judge is a right dog' **3.** (CRS) the telephone. Dog and bone = phone **4.** a cigarette butt **5.** to follow **6.** (Aus) police informer.

DOG EYE; lookout on a team of three-card-tricksters. See also *keep dog*.

DOGGIE FASHION; heterosexual intercourse with the man covering the woman from the rear. Not anal intercourse.

DOGS; the tumblers of a safe.

DOG'S COCK; a sausage.

DO IT YOURSELF KIT; masturbation.

DONE A SLAMMER; to have been cautioned by the police as a juvenile.

DONG; a penis.

DONNIKER; lavatory, often an outside one. Corruption of 18c word dunnaken. Now more commonly used in America and Australia along with variant *dunny*.

DOOJEE; heroin.

DO ONE'S LOT, to; to lose all one's money.

DOPE; 1. any narcotic **2.** information (particularly about a horse or dog race).

DOSE; 1. gonorrhoea **2.** a prison sentence.

DOSH; (West African 18c) money, a tip or a bribe.

DOSSER; 1. a tramp or someone who sleeps rough. From 18c doss or dorse meaning bed. or **2.** north London children's slang for any drug taker.

DO THE BUSINESS, to; 1. to kill **2.** to complete a crime successfully **3.** to bribe a police officer **4.** to have sexual intercourse.

DOUBLE A MARK; to steal or beg twice from a person in quick succession.

DOUBLE BOAT; (UK) an elderly person who does not have all his or her faculties. Originally a code expression of a small group of criminals.

DOUBLE CARPET; betting term for a horse or dog at odds of 33-1.

DOUBLE IN THE BUBBLE; a call in a game of craps indicating that for certain numbers odds of 2-1 instead of even money will be paid for a winning throw.

DOUBLE SAWBUCK; (Can) ten-year prison sentence.

DOUBLE THE MELT, to; to have two successive orgasms without withdrawal.

DOWN, to go d. on; to engage in oral intercourse.

DOWNHILL; the last half of a prison sentence.

DQ; detention quarters, naval prison.

D-RACKS; cards.

DRAG; 1. the street **2.** prison sentence of three months **3.** car or van **4.** a share or percentage.

DRAG, in; dressing in the clothing of the other sex. In operas when the maid appears as a boy this is delicately referred to as a 'trouser role'.

DRAGGING; stealing from motor vehicles.

DRAW; cannabis.

DRECK; (Yiddish) literally ordure, now meaning **1.** an unpleasant person or **2.** anything shoddy or poorly made.

DRINK; 1. a term used in mitigation to indicate only minor benefit from a crime, as in 'All I got out of it was a drink.' Probably up to about £25, as opposed to a *big drink* which starts in the hundreds and is offered as an inducement, eg 'If he rings the bell (qv) there'll be a big drink in it for him' **2.** a bribe.

DRIP, to; to complain or grumble.

DROP; a place where money or information is left to be collected at a later time.

DROP, or **THE LONG DROP;** death by hanging.

DROP ANCHOR IN BUM BAY, to; to have anal intercourse.

DROPPER; a passer of forged notes.

DROPSY; bribery, particularly relating to the police.

DROWNING; obtaining entry into an old person's house by pretending to be from the Water Board. (Also: 'Gassing' and 'Electrocuting'.)

DRUM; 1. a house or flat **2.** (Can) prison cell.

DRUMMER; a clerk in a solicitor's office who is able to attract clients.

DRUMMING; 1. stealing from flats and houses after ringing the bell to ensure the occupant is out **2.** obtaining work for a solicitor. A clerk will either be able to do this through contacts, going out drinking with clients, or by spreading a little (or a lot) of money around police stations so that recommendations are made to him when clients ask the arresting officer if he knows a good brief (qv).

DRY BATH; search of a prison cell by warders.

DUBBED UP, to be; (Glas) to be locked up, in prison.

DUCK AND DIVE, to; to make a scratchy living not necessarily in a totally honest way. In context: 'How've you been?' 'I've been ducking and diving.' As 'bobbing and weaving', which comes from the action of a skilful boxer who avoids a blow.

DUFF; 1. badly made, faulty, **2.** incorrect, as in 'All he does is give duff info.'

DUFF UP, to; to beat up.

DUKES; (RS) fists. Duke of Yorks = forks = fingers.

DUMMY, to beat the; to masturbate.

DUMMY UP, to; to remain silent during police questioning.

DUN, to; to pursue a debt.

DUNNY; (Aus) lavatory. See also *donniker*.

DUNS; bailiffs.

DYNAMITE; any narcotic of high potency.

E

E; ecstasy. A mixture of cocaine and LSD. Stimulant drug said to loosen sexual inhibitions and improve performance.

EAGLE; a winning player in a card game.

EAR; a bent corner put on a playing card to identify it.

EARN, to; to obtain money in a slightly dishonest way, probably through ducking and diving (qv).

EARNER; the opportunity to make a profit from a slightly dishonest deal.

EASY; 1. easily seduced **2.** indifferent, as in 'Do you want to go to the cinema?' 'I'm easy.' 'I know but I asked if you wanted to go to the cinema.'

EASY LAY; a girl who can be relied on to have intercourse at the end of an evening in return for dinner or a few drinks.

EASY RIDER; a pimp, particularly a good one. Originally turn-of-the-century black slang but now widespread after the film of the same name.

EAT, to; to perform fellatio.

EAT PUSSY, to; to perform cunnilingus.

EDGE: 1. an advantage **2.** (Scots) look-out, as in 'Keeping the edge up'.

EGYPTIAN PT; (Army) sleep.

EIGHT BALL; a negro, from the fact that the eight ball in a pool game is black.

EIGHTH; the quantity in which drugs are sold and valued at street level, eg 'He sold me an eighth for £10'.

ELBOW; 1. (US west coast) a policeman **2.** part of a pickpocket team, the man who distracts the victim.

ELBOW BENDER; a hard drinker.

ELBOW, on the; see *bow, on the.*

ELEPHANT; (RS) anus. From elephant and castle = arsehole.

ELIMINATE, to 1. to kill **2.** to pass body waste.

END; 1. share in the proceeds of a theft or to have sexual intercourse, as in 'Are you getting your end away?' **2.** the best, an example of **value** reversal.

ENFORCER; a sledgehammer. (Flying Squad term).

EQUALISER; a gun.

ERASE; to murder.

EXES; 1. a prison sentence of six months. Back slang even if slightly misspelt **2.** six pounds.

EXPERIENCE; an LSD or mescaline experience.

EXTRAS; the additional, and this time sexual, services provided in a massage parlour.

EYE; a detective, from the Pinkerton detective agency symbol of the open eye.

F; (US) $50 bill.

FACE; a known criminal. Before the coming of the Crown Prosecution Service when a known local villain was arrested young police officers were sent to court on his first appearance to see which 'faces' turned up in the public gallery to watch the proceedings, so that a tenuous link could be established between them and the accused.

FACTORY; police station.

FADE, to; 1. to hurry away on arrival of the police **2.** loss of position by a horse in the last stages of a race.

FAG; 1. a cigarette **2.** a male homosexual. There are a number of versions of its derivation. One is that it was used in the First World War when cigarettes were considered effeminate by pipe and cigar smokers. A second possible origin is from the 'fags', the first year boys at British public schools who performed menial tasks for older boys and who, it was traditionally supposed, serviced them sexually **3.** originally, in criminal slang, a pickpocket.

FAG-HAG; (US) woman who associates with homosexuals.

FAIRY; male homosexual.

FALCONER; a con-man posing as an aristocrat.

FALL; an arrest.

FALL, to; to become pregnant.

FALL GUY; a person designated by other members of a gang to be arrested for a crime.

FALL MONEY; cash set aside to pay a lawyer in the event of arrest.

FAMILY JEWELS;
testicles. A term often used by
boxers.

FAN, to; to undertake a quick
check of clothing for concealed
valuables.

FANNING; pickpocketing.

FANNY; (UK) **1.** the vagina
2. nonsense, as in 'Don't try to
fanny me' **3.** (US) backside, as
in 'He fell flat on his fanny.'

FANNY ADAMS, Sweet;
1. euphemism for *fuck all* **2.**
(Navy) a cylindrical mess tin
holding about a gallon. Originally
it contained tinned meat and
when introduced in the late
1860s it was not popular. Shortly
after its introduction a solicitor's
clerk murdered and
dismembered a child called
Fanny Adams at Alton,
Hampshire. The standing joke
was that the tinned meat was the
remains of the child.

FARTLEBERRIES; the
pellets of faeces which cling to
the hairs of the anus and defy
dislodgement. Old English, and

would have been considered
obsolete had not a folk band
toured under the name in the
1960s.

FAT; having a good supply of
narcotics.

**FAT LADY SINGS, the
opera's not over until the;**
(US) defeat is not yet inevitable.
There is still time for something
to happen. The expression used
sometimes is 'The fat lady hasn't
sung yet.'

FAT MAN, the; (USbl) the
electric chair.

FAW; a Gypsy. A Scottish clan
of gypsies had the surname Faa,
and the word faw is extant in the
north of England.

FEEL, to cop a; to touch a
woman's sexual parts.

FEELER; a gentle enquiry
made to see if arrangements can
be made with the police over bail
and other matters.

FENCE; a receiver of stolen
goods.

FERRET, to exercise the;
(Aus) to have sexual intercourse.

FIFTEEN ROUND BOUT;
long sex session. For safety
reasons almost all boxing
championships are now boxed
over 12 rounds.

FILE; a pickpocket.

FILTER, to; to desert.

FILTH; the police.

FIN; 1. five dollars **2.** (Can) five-year prison sentence.

FIND THE LADY; variation of the three-card trick.

FINEST; sarcastic term for the police as in 'London's finest' or 'New York's finest'.

FINGER, to; to give information to the police, naming names.

FINGER PIE; stimulation of the clitoris.

FINGER WAVE; anal examination for drugs.

FINISHING SCHOOL; Borstal or sometimes a women's prison.

FINK, or **RATFINK; 1.** any unpleasant and untrustworthy person, formerly a private policeman hired by a mine or factory to break a strike. Fink was originally pink, a contraction of Pinkerton who ran a detective agency and hired out men for strike breaking **2.** a police informer.

FIRE PROOFER; (US) a confidence trickster who preys on the religious. From the proximity of hell fire.

FIRM; a gang **1.** of organised criminals. The Flying Squad was once said to contain a 'firm within a firm' **2.** of football hooligans.

FIRMING; a gang beating-up.

FIRST BASE; a teenage expression indicating the touching of a girl's breasts on a date. To qualify fully there had to be flesh on flesh not mere touching her jumper. Second base was to touch her pudenda. The term comes from the progression around the bases in baseball. Other versions of the progression suggest that first base need only be open-mouthed kissing. The progress could be discussed subsequently amongst the boy's male friends.

FIRST BIRD; the first time in prison.

FISH; a new inmate in prison, sometimes called *fresh fish*.

FIST FUCK; to insert the hand and wrist into the sexual partner's anus or vagina. Particularly common amongst homosexuals attracted to sado-masochism. The practice can result in severe internal injuries.

FITTED; badly beaten, as in 'I fitted him.' Short for 'I fitted him for his coffin.'

FIT UP, to; to plant or give false evidence to ensure a conviction.

FIX, the; the result of *fix, to 1.* so the outcome of a race or boxing bout is predetermined.

FIX, to; 1. to arrange by bribery or threats **2.** to inject a drug.

FIZGIG; (Aus) a police informer.

FLADGE AND PADGE; flagellation and pageantry. Bondage and dressing-up for sexual titillation.

FLAKE OUT; to go to sleep. From the method of feeding out a rope laying it flat in long form.

FLAKEY; 1. scary **2.** mentally unstable.

FLAPPING TRACK; an unlicenced greyhound track where dogs are run under aliases. In theory a dog which has run on such a track cannot run on a licenced track but in practice there is a steady two-way trade of runners. The principal reason for running dogs in such places is for betting purposes but they are sometimes used in training.

FLASH; the effect of cocaine and to lesser extent methedrine.

FLASHER; indecent exposer.

FLATBACKER; part-time prostitute.

FLATBACKS; (Army) term of derision for personnel.

FLATFOOT; policeman, especially uniformed.

FLIM; 1. five pound note **2.** a five-year sentence.

FLIM-FLAM, to; to cheat or swindle, therefore Flim-flam man = con-man.

FLIT, to; 1. leave often in a hurry without paying rent. See also *moonlight*. **2.** (US) homosexual, college slang from the 1950s.

FLOATER; (Aus) meat pie in pea soup, a cultural delicacy.

FLOG, to; to sell.

FLOG ONE'S MEAT, to; to masturbate.

FLOWERY (DELL); prison cell. Originates from an old song 'Peter Bell'.

FLUSHING; drawing blood back into the syringe when taking drugs.

FLY; clever.

FLY, on the; in a hurry. Ice hockey players are said to change 'on the fly' when they vault the boards and enter the game mid-play to substitute for another player.

FLYNN, in like; to take up an opportunity or invitation as in 'He was in like Flynn.' Often used in sexual terms and deriving from the alleged sexual enthusiasm shown by the Australian actor Errol Flynn.

FOLD, to; to give up suddenly in a card game or a boxing match; sometimes, in the latter, by arrangement, eg 'He'll fold in the third.'

FOLDING STUFF; paper money as opposed to coins.

FOLLIES; quarter sessions. Not used nowadays for the Crown Court.

FORK; (RS) the hand. Duke of Yorks = forks = fingers.

FORM; 1. previous criminal convictions **2.** the previous running of a horse or greyhound.

FOX; a girl or woman. Originally black use but now common amongst other groups such as bikers.

FOXY; sexy. Same derivation as fox.

FRAME, to; to obtain a conviction by false evidence.

FRAME, to be in the; 1. to be suspected of a crime **2.** to be left money in a will. From the practice of putting the numbers of winning horses in a frame.

FREEBIE; something obtained without payment especially a ticket or sex with a prostitute.

FREELOADER; a person who gatecrashes parties or receptions and so obtains free food and drink.

FRENCH; oral sex.

FRIG, to; to have sexual intercourse. Frigging is often used as a euphemism for fucking.

FRIG ABOUT, to; to fool or play about. Friggers are pieces of glass such as walking sticks or rolling pins blown by 19c apprentices at England's Nailsea glassworks in their spare time.

FRIGHTENER; a man sent round to debtors, particularly of bookmakers, to enforce payment by threats. Sometimes a man employed to persuade a witness to change his or her evidence.

FRISK, to; 1. to search quickly for drugs, stolen goods or concealed weapons. The word is 18c in its origin and comes from the gambolling of a lamb. **2.** (US) to pickpocket.

FRONT; 1. the person on view to the police and public shielding the real owners of a dishonest business. Fronts very often have no criminal record which makes conviction difficult, and even where there is a conviction it is often followed by a light sentence. See also *long firm* **2.** to put a suspect face-to-face with his identifier, an abbreviation of confront **3.** the main street.

FRONT THE GAFF, to; to go to the main door of a large house with a view to committing a burglary.

FROTTAGE; rubbing up against women in crowded places. See also *bustle pinching*.

FRUIT; homosexual. Question: Why is San Francisco like a Hershey bar? Answer: Because it's full of fruits, flakes and nuts.

FRUIT FLY; woman, not necessarily lesbian, who associates with male homosexuals.

FRY, to; to be electrocuted in the electric chair.

FUCK, to; 1. to have sexual intercourse **2.** to cheat or trick.

FUCK ABOUT, to; to be a nuisance, as in 'Don't fuck about.'

FUCK-UP; terrible mistake.

FUDGE PACKER; (Can) homosexual.

FULL; full of drugs.

FULL HOUSE; to have either both head and body lice or to have both syphillis and gonorrhoea.

FUNNY FARM; mental hospital.

FURBURGER, to eat a; cunnilingus.

FUTURE; the testicles. A common graffitti in men's public lavatories is: The future of Britain is in your hands.'

FUZZ; (US) police. Possibly because they make a 'fuss' about crime. Originally American east coast slang taken up by hippies and now in general use.

G

G; 1. (UK) £1000 but never really common **2.** (US) $1000 **3.** (US) a gun as in a G-man.

GABBER; a policeman. A corruption of *gavver* (qv).

GAFF; 1. a house or flat **2.** an aid to cheating in gambling **3.** any sort of swindle. There was a considerable hierarchy in the carnival world depending on whether gaffs were used to deceive the punters. A Fat Lady, eg, could be said to be non-gaffed and therefore at the top of the social tree; whereas the Half Man-Half Woman would have to resort to gaffs to maintain the illusion, eg with depilatories, over-exercise of one half of the body, possibly a false breast.

GALLOUS; (Scots) flashy, hard, smart.

GAM; 1. fellatio **2.** a leg. Originally an ill-formed or spindly one, now applied to legs in general.

GAME; 1. smart but full of courage. Bareknuckle boxers were often described as game. The word is now in common usage and often means the willingness to expose oneself to ridicule, as in the television show 'Game for a Laugh' **2.** Open to bribery, as in 'Is he game?' In the 19c and early 20c game meant dishonest, and even earlier a *game pullet* was the term for a young prostitute.

GAME, on the; engaged in prostitution.

GAMMY; lame. From the use of gam as a leg.

GANGBANG; multiple rape.

GANGBANGER; member of street gang in Los Angeles.

GARTER; (US) an indeterminate sentence which may be lengthened or shortened.

GASH; 1. the mouth **2.** a prostitute **3.** a woman but considered only in the sexual sense, as in 'Had any gash recently?' **4.** (US) a white woman who has been raped **5.** rubbish.

GASHBIN; a dustbin.

GASSING; obtaining entrance to flats and houses of the elderly by pretending to be from the Gas Board.

GATE; the money collected from spectators at an event.

GATE ARREST; the immediate re-arrest for an outstanding offence of a prisoner as he leaves the prison gates at the end of his sentence. Something bitterly disliked and feared by inmates. The threat of this process can be used by the police as a means of persuading suspects to admit on initial arrest to outstanding crimes and have these taken into consideration by the judge. The advantages are mutual. The accused very often gets credit for his frankness and little, if anything, added to his sentence. The police clear up their books.

GATE FEVER; the emotion shown by prisoners nearing the end of their sentence.

GAVVERS; police (probably from the Romany).

GAY BASHING; (US) beating up homosexuals. Known as queer-bashing (qv) in Britain.

GAY DECEIVERS; false breasts worn by flat-chested women.

GEAR; 1. clothing **2.** drugs. The story is told of Allan Green, Director of Public Prosecutions who, while cross-examining in a careless driving case at Highgate Magistrates' Court during his early days at the Bar asked a motorist what gear he was in. 'Me usual,' came the reply, 'me studs and leathers.'

GEEK; (US) a freak, very often a fake, in a carnival or circus show who would perform disgusting acts such as biting the head off a live chicken or snake. The term is said to have been first used by a man named Wagner from West Virginia. The act itself would not be on public display but would be an extra, rather as some murals at Pompeii were shown to gentlemen only after the main tour. There was often a considerable amount of gaff used. After all, live chickens cost money. Now used as a term of abuse.

GELT; money.

GEMMIE; (Glas) a hard man.

GET; see *git*.

GETS; an escape from prison.

GET TO, to; to be in a position to bribe a policeman, juror, greyhound trainer etc.

GIMP; a lame person. Originally someone with a bad leg but now used of personality defects as well.

GIMPY; lame.

GIN AND JAGUAR BELT; Smart districts of Surrey, England, and suitable targets for professional house-breaking exercises.

GIN AND JAGUAR BIRD; married woman from the above not averse to extra-marital intercourse.

GINGER; 1. (CRS) homosexual, as in 'Is he ginger?' Ginger beer = queer **2.** (Aus) a prostitute's client.

GIN-MILL; saloon or bar.

GIT; a bastard. Used now as a general term of abuse. One

derivation is that is comes from 'one of his get or offspring'; another that it is a stockbreeding term for the offspring sired by a stray stallion that has mixed in with a group of mares.

GIVE IT A SPIN, to; 1. to search **2.** to attempt.

GIVE IT THE BIG 'UN, to; 1. to boast or brag **2.** to intimidate.

GIVEN A LIFE, to be; to be searched by the police and later released.

GIZZIT; a free handout such as a ballpoint pen for promotional purposes. The derivation is from *Give us it*.

GLASGOW HELLO; see *Glasgow kiss*.

GLASGOW KISS; a headbutt.

GLASS; the penis.

GLASS, to blow his; fellatio.

GLASSHOUSE; military detention, from a building at North Camp, Aldershot, England, which had a large glass roof and was used as a prison.

GLASSJAW; said of a boxer with an inability to withstand a punch to the chin. See also *roundheels*.

GLIM; a match, or a light.

GLORY, get the; used of a prisoner who has turned religious either genuinely or in hope of getting preferential treatment. Also known as *got the book*.

GOBBLE, to; oral sex, particularly between males.

GOBBLER'S GULCH; homosexual rendez-vous. One

such is an area on Primrose Hill, near Regent's Park, London.

GOD BOTHERER; clergyman of any description but particularly an Anglican or a Methodist.

GO DOWN; 1. to be convicted and sentenced to a term of imprisonment **2.** to participate in oral sex.

GOFER; a lackey, someone who goes for this and goes for that.

GOFFER; (Navy) a non-alcoholic drink, often used merely as non-spiritous.

GOING QE; (literally going Queen's Evidence) giving evidence for the prosecution against former colleagues in return for immunity from prosecution or a lighter sentence.

GOLD AND SILVER; bisexual.

GOLD BRICKING; malingering, principally an army term. Origin is in the 1860s when the gold brick game was a straight forward swindle where the mug was induced to lend money in the belief that the security offered was a genuine bar of gold. A gold bricker was therefore a fraud. It is also the term used for someone who feigns illness to avoid duty.

GOLDEN SHOWER; a service offered by prostitutes who will accept being urinated upon by, or will urinate on, clients.

GONIFF; a small time thief.

GONK; a prostitute's client.

GONSIL; 1. a young thief **2.** punk (qv) or catamite.

GOOD TIME; (Can) remission.

GOOF; (Can) a convict. The worst possible term of abuse amongst prisoners.

GOOF, to; 1. to give oneself up to the police **2.** to spoil an injection of a narcotic **3.** to make a mistake.

GOOF BALLS; barbiturates.

GOOLIES; testicles. From the Hindi *goolies* = a round object.

GOOLIES, to have someone by the; to have the upper hand. A person with his testicles in a grip is in no position to argue.

GOON SQUAD; (Can) prison riot squad.

GO OVER THE WALL; escape from prison.

GORILLA; a hard man, the enforcer on a team, a violent person.

GOT THE BOOK; see *glory, got the.*

GRAB, to; to arrest.

GRAFT; 1. bribery **2.** to work hard.

GRAFTER; 1. pickpocket **2.** a hard worker.

GRAND; £1000 or $1000.

GRANNY; a legitimate business used to cover dishonesty, particularly the disposal of stolen goods.

GRASS; 1. police informer **2.** cannabis.

GRASS EATER; a policeman who will accept bribes but who will not actively look for them.

GRASSHOPPER; (RS) policeman. Grasshopper = copper.

GRAVEYARD SHIFT; the early morning turn as dealer or croupier in a casino when there are few punters about and the place is as quiet as the proverbial graveyard.

GRAVY, to dish out; hand out heavy sentences. See also *dish out the porridge.*

GRAVY TRAIN; success, the good times.

GREEK; anal intercourse, as in the negative 'I don't do Greek'. From the Greek's alleged predeliction for that form of intercourse.

GREEN AND BLACKS; librium capsules.

GREEN RUB; a piece of bad luck. From the green discharge produced when a masturbator has gonorrhoea.

GREENS; sex in the abstract, as in 'Are you getting your greens?'

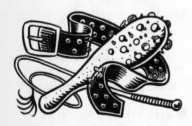

GREET, to; (Scots) to cry.

GREYMAN; (WI) a white person.

GRIEF; inconvenience.

GRIFT, to; (US) to steal.

GRIPPO; (Navy) an invitation to a sailor in a foreign port to go to the home of a resident, as in 'I got a grippo last night.' In the mess it can mean an invitation to tea. Below decks it almost invariably refers to sexual intercourse.

GROIN; a diamond ring.

GROOVY; (Glas) a scar.

GROYNE; see *groin.*

GRUMBLE, to have a bit of; (RS) sexual intercourse. Grumble and grunt = cunt.

GRUNT; an American infantry soldier.

GRUNT AND GROANER; professional wrestler, from the noises made by the contestants partly for balance and partly to simulate pain.

GRUNTER; (Aus) young girl, used with sexual connotations.

GULPERS; (Navy) a large favour. It comes from naval usage when if a favour was to be asked it was repaid by either a sip or a gulp of the daily tot of rum, or, in extreme cases, the whole tot. Even now, with the abolition of the tot, the debt is repaid in drink not money.

GUN; 1. (US) a pickpocket **2.** a syringe.

GUN, to; to accelerate sharply, as in 'He gunned the motor.'

GUN SHY; cowardly. Often used of dogs being trained to the gun who become panicky at the sound of shooting.

GUNSIL; see *gonsil*.

GUY THE COURSE, to; (Glas) to run away.

GUZZLING THE GRASS; (Aus) vomiting.

H

H; heroin.

HABIT; a drug addiction.

HACK UP, to; to win easily, from racing.

HAIRCUT; short prison sentence.

HAIR PIE; cunnilingus.

HAIRY; dangerous.

HALF A BAR; 50p.

HALF AND HALF; 1. prostitute's service of half oral and half ordinary sexual intercourse **2.** service in a massage parlour where for part of the time the customer is allowed to massage the girl.

HALF A STRETCH; six months' imprisonment.

HALF A TON; £50.

HALF BRASS; a girl who will hand out sexual favours freely and does not accept money.

HALF IRON; a bisexual.

HALF OF MARGE; (RS) police sergeant.

HAMPTON; (RS) penis. Hampton Wick = prick. Usually used as a term of derision as in 'He's a right Hampton' rather than 'My Hampton's sore.'

HANDFUL; 1. five pounds **2.** five-year prison sentence **3.** five lengths (racing).

HAND JOB; masturbation, often by another party, eg in a massage parlour.

HAND SHANDY; masturbation.

HANDS UP, to put your; to plead guilty, to confess all.

HANGER HOOKS; hooks sewn into the lining of clothing worn by professional shoplifters.

HANGING JUDGE; one who will favour the prosecution to ensure a conviction and will then impose a harsh sentence.

Mr Justice Avory had the reputation for that sort of conduct in the 1920s. It is said that on his arrival for the assizes at Winchester, he tipped the porter sixpence for carrying his bags. 'Is that all?' asked the man. 'You're lucky,' replied Avory, 'the last time I was here I gave a man seven years.' The original hanging judge seems to have been Judge Roy Bean, known as The Law West of the Pecos, of Langtry, Texas, a town named by him after The Jersey Lily.

HANS CHRISTIAN ANDERSEN; a police officer who invents verbals (qv) or fairy tales.

HAPPY DUST; cocaine.

HARD; chewing tobacco.

HARD ON, to have a; to have an erection.

HARDWARE; weapons.

HARD WAY; a sentence served without remission. The use of this expression formed part of the evidence against James Hanratty, convicted of England's A6 murder. In the conversation the murderer is said to have used the expression relating to a Borstal sentence. Hanratty had served one and had been deprived of remission because of his bad conduct.

HAROLD; celluloid, from the name of the silent film star, Harold Lloyd.

HARP; 1. harmonica **2.** Irish immigrant to America.

HASH; hashish.

HAT; $25. A bribe or gratuity often given to a police officer for information.

HATCHET MAN; hired killer. From the use by the Tong killers of the hatchet – a combination of an axe and a hammer.

HAUL ASS; (US) to leave, often in a hurry.

HAVE IT, to; to accept an accusation, to plead guilty.

HAVE IT AWAY, to; 1. to successfully complete a crime **2.** to escape from the police **3.** to have sexual intercourse.

HAVE IT OFF, to; see *have it away*.

HAVE IT ON ONE'S TOES, to; to escape from the police.

HAVE ONE'S COLLAR FELT, to; to be arrested.

HAWKSHAW; (WI) the police.

HAW MAWS; (Glas) testicles.

H.B.I.; (UK) house breaking instruments.

HEAD, to give; to fellate.

HEADS; (Navy) the lavatory, said to derive from the lavatory being at the head of a sailing vessel. Another version of the origin is that barrels constructed with seats were put over the side. When the defecators sat in them only their heads were visible.

HEAP; an old motor vehicle.

HEAP CLOUTING; motor vehicle stealing.

HEAT; 1. the police and therefore **2.** trouble **3.** a gun.

HEAVE; to be sick.

HEAVE HO, to get the old; 1. to be dismissed from employment. Usually used in connection with the misfortune of others. 'Tommy had the old heave ho last week' rather than 'I got the heave ho' **2.** to be ejected from a dance hall or cinema **3.** to be rejected by a lover.

HEAVY; 1. a major criminal **2.** a Flying Squad car, usually used in the plural.

HEAVY MOB; Flying, Robbery or Serious Crime squads.

HEDGE; the crowd around a street salesman or three-card trick game.

HEEL; sneak thief.

HEEL-TAP; a small amount of liquid left in a glass. In naval and military messes it is often considered bad form when drinking a toast to leave a heel-tap. 'No heel-taps, gentlemen.'

HE-ING AND SHE-ING; sexual intercourse.

HEIST; a corruption of hoist; a robbery, often a highjacking.

HICKEY; a love bite.

HIGH FIVES; palm slapping salute with hand held in the air. Originally used as a greeting amongst black youths but now adopted by sportsmen after a goal or, home run has been scored.

HIGH JACK, to; to commit a robbery usually stealing a lorry full of goods and then dumping the lorry. One version of the origin stems from the tendency of Americans to call strangers 'Jack'. In the days of prohibition the robber would tell the driver to raise his arms. 'High, Jack.'

HIGH OFF THE HOG; living well, from the best cut of pork.

HIT, to make a; 1. to kill **2.** to make a quick profit at cards or dice **3.** to dilute drugs prior to selling them **4.** to obtain drugs **5.** to borrow money.

HIT THE BRICKS, to; 1. to go out-of-doors and specifically **2.** to be released from prison.

HIT THE TOE, to; (Aus) to abscond, run away.

HOBO; (US) a tramp. There are a number of suggestions for the origin and probably the best is that it derives from the call 'Here boy'. Another is the suggestion that as he begs food in a wheedling tone he resembles an oboe. A third is that soldiers returning from the American Civil War, when asked where they were going, replied '*Ho*meward *Bo*und'. Yet another is that it derives from hoe-boy from the work given to an itinerant labourer.

HOISTER; a shoplifter, usually female.

HOLE, the; the punishment cell in many American prisons. Although the actual size varied, the one at Soledad, measuring just over 8′ by 6′, was fairly typical. The prisoner was kept naked with food pushed under the door. There was no light.

HOLLOW TOOTH; New Scotland Yard. Used by disgruntled police officers.

HOME AND COLONIAL; Regional Crime Squad, from the chain of grocery stores.

HONEYMAN; the cess pit cleaner.

HONEY POT; (Can) prison lavatory.

HONK, to; to vomit.

HONKY; (US) a white person. Originally a term of abuse now more freely used.

HOOCH; (Can) illicit prison liquor. In the wider world specifically whisky. The derivation is from the American Indian *hoocheno* = liquor.

HOOD; male criminal engaged in professional crime. The word is an abbreviation of *hoodlum* which itself may have been a corruption of Hoodler, the name of some particularly unpleasant brothers from San Francisco in the 1860s. Another version of its origin is that it arose from the mugger's practice of turning up the collar and lapels of his jacket or coat before a mugging took place, thereby making identification more difficult.

HOOK; 1. a thief, specifically a pickpocket. From the old use of the word for fingers **2.** a bent pin used for injecting narcotics.

HOOKER; a prostitute; named after General Hooker, an American Civil War soldier who encouraged females to follow the camp. Another version is that it is slightly earlier and originates from the Dutch *hoeker* = huckster. A third that it derives from an expression referring to an inhabitant of The Hook, a brothel area used by sailors in New York in the late 1850s. It is possible all three derivations are correct.

HOOKING; 1. prostitution **2.** attempting to smear the police by making false accusations.

HOOTER; the nose.

HOOTERS; the breasts.

HOP; opium.

HOP-HEAD; drug addict.

HORN; 1. the telephone **2.** the erect penis.

HORNY; sexually aroused, applicable to either sex.

HORSE; 1. heroin **2.** a prison warder who will smuggle letters and other goods in and out of prison **3.** (RS) Gonorrhoea. Horse and trap = clap.

HORSE'S ASS; a fool, often used self-deprecatingly.

HORSE'S COCK; (Can) sausages.

HOSE JOB; oral sex.

HOSS; (north Yorkshire) a woman, as in 'Not a bad lookin' 'oss'.

HOT; 1. stolen **2.** wanted by the police **3.** talented, as in 'I want a brief who's a bit hot'. In this last instance an abbreviation of *shit hot*.

HOTEL; 1. police station as opposed to the cells **2.** Strangeways prison is known as The Hotel.

HOT-LOT; either the Flying Squad or Special Patrol Group.

HOT-SEAT; the electric chair.

HOT-SEAT, to be in the; to be in difficulties or an unpleasant position.

HOT SQUAT; the electric chair.

HOUSE; a brothel, as in 'A house is not a home'.

HOUSE, to; to follow to a flat, house or garage, to discover stolen property.

HUCKLE, to; (Glas) to arrest, apprehend.

HUMP, to; (UK) to have sexual intercourse. Originally 18c but still in fairly common use.

HUMPTY; sexual intercourse.

HURT, to; to need drugs.

HUSTLE, to; originally **1.** to commit a robbery but now more usually **2.** to obtain dishonestly and specifically **3.** to obtain a bet by falsely making the odds look attractive to the punter, eg by purposely playing pool or cards badly until the stakes are raised **4.** to practise prostitution.

HUSTLER; 1. prostitute of either sex **2.** a player who will deliberately make himself look bad at pool, cards etc to increase the stakes when he will show his true ability.

HYPE; hypodermic needle.

I

ICE; 1. diamonds **2.** money paid to police to allow an illegal gambling or drinking club to stay open. So called because it takes the heat off **3.** extra payment to obtain a benefit.

ICE, to; to kill.

ICEBOX, in the; to be in solitary confinement in prison.

ICE CREAM; narcotic.

ICE MAN; 1. a professional killer and therefore, in the abstract, death **2.** person who pays out the protection money. See also *bagman* **3.** jewel thief.

I.D.B.; illicit diamond buying.

IDIOT BOX; the television.

ID PARADE; literally identification parade, line-up conducted to establish whether a witness can recognise a suspect standing in a parade of eight people. Thought in Britain to be the safest way of obtaining identification evidence. Other alternatives include the group identification when the suspect is placed in the car park of a public house or on the escalator at an underground station, or in a face to face confrontation with the witness.

IFFY; 1. a risky undertaking, as in 'It's a bit iffy.' Something if not illegal certainly not legal **2.** stolen or dishonestly obtained goods, as in 'They're a bit iffy'.

IKEY MO; derogatory term for Jewish person, a contraction of Isaac Moses.

ILLYWHACKER; (Aus) a swindler.

IN, the; 1. an entrée **2.** influence.

INSIDE; in prison.

INSIDE JOB; a robbery or theft which can only have taken place with the co-operation of either the owner of the business (for insurance purposes) or the staff.

IRISH WAY; heterosexual anal intercourse; used to prevent pregnancy and to avoid the sin of coitus interruptus. No mention is made of the sin of sodomy.

IRON; 1. (RS) homosexual. Iron hoof = poof; originally a male prostitute but now in more general use **2.** a firearm.

IRON OUT, to; to solve a problem. From the use of the iron to take wrinkles out of clothing. In slang the phrase formerly meant to kill.

IRONS; knuckledusters.

ISLAND, the; Isle of Wight specifically Parkhurst prison. Because of the difficult currents surrounding it, it is said that no one has ever made a successful

escape from the island. The same applies to the now disused Alcatraz prison in San Francisco Bay.

ITALIAN FOOTBALL; a bomb.

IT LOOKS LIKE RAIN; an arrest is imminent.

IVORIES; 1. teeth, from boxing **2.** piano keys **3.** dice.

J

JACK; 1. (UK) erection, as in 'I had a jack up to my eyebrows'. From ejaculate **2.** to copulate **3.** policeman, or detective. When the Liverpool (where the word is common) police were investigating the Wallace murder in 1920, in which much was made of the time taken to walk a particular route, they were called Springheeled Jacks because of the speed with which they covered the ground, to the advantage of the prosecution. *Springheeled Jack* was a well known Victorian melodrama, the title role of which was often played by the actor Tod Slaughter who specialised in villainous parts **4.** (UK) five pounds. Usually used in the plural, and from the rhyming slang, Jack's alive = five **5.** (UK) heroin; from the rhyming slang Jack and Jill = pill **6.** (RS) Alone, as in 'He's on his jack'. Jack Jones = alone.

JACK IN THE BOX; 1. (US) house-breaking **2.** (Bl) the sexual position of having the penis in the vagina.

JACK IT IN; (UK) **1.** to stop **2.** to retire. Often used as a command to someone being quarrelsome, as in 'Jack it in.'

JACK OFF; 1. (UK) masturbate **2.** (US) pumping the plunger of a hypodermic needle backwards and forwards to resemble masturbation.

JACK ROLLER; (US) mugger of homosexuals and tramps, and particularly drunks. One of the most respected biographies of a criminal is *Memoirs of a Jack Roller* written in the 1920s and one which is often cited as a classic example of research.

JACK THE LAD; a boaster or show off, as in 'Don't come Jack the lad with me'. The term

is often used with some admiration on the part of the speaker, as in 'He's a right Jack the lad.'

JACK-UP, to; 1. to increase the price **2.** (Aus) to plead not guilty **3.** to refuse.

JAG; a bout of drinking.

JAILBAIT; sexually precocious girl under the age of consent. Also known by such names as *San Quentin Quail* from the prison sentence which would follow sexual intercourse. A remark made to someone eyeing a young girl was 'Fourteen gets you three.' Now more likely probation.

JAKE; 1. methylated spirits **2.** (US) all right, as in 'Everything's Jake' **3.** a uniformed police officer.

JAKES; a lavatory. Originating in the 16c it is now principally of naval usage.

JAM; (USbl) **1.** cocaine **2.** homosexual foreplay **3.** the vagina **4.** (UK) semen **5.** term for a heterosexual man used by homosexuals.

JAM BUTTY; (UK) police car. This may be from the Cockney rhyming slang, jam jar = car, but more likely from the red-stripe-on-white sported by some police force vehicles.

JAM FAG; (US) homosexual with no other real interest in life.

JAM-JAR; (CRS) motor car, used especially of a police car.

JAM RAGS; sanitary towels.

JAM ROLL; (CRS) parole.

JANG; the penis.

JARGOON; a fake diamond ring used for the purposes of deception.

J ARTHUR; 1. (UK RS) masturbation, from J Arthur Rank (the film mogul) = wank. It is said that the film *The Bofors Gun* was refused distribution on the Rank circuit because one of the characters says 'I'm off to have a J. Arthur'. **2.** bank.

JAY; marijuana cigarette.

JAZZ; 1. the vagina **2.** sexual intercourse. It is interesting how the word came into common use meaning to speed things up. This allowed for tunes with titles such as 'Jazz me baby' and 'Don't give me none of that jazz' to be played with impunity.

JELLY-ROLL; (USbl) **1.** the vulva **2.** sexual intercourse generally. The pianist Ferdinand Morton was known as 'Jelly Roll' because of his enthusiasm for both **3.** an easy and enjoyable task.

JERK; 1. originally a short branch line on a railway **2.** a masturbator from *jerk off*. This has fallen into disuse and the word is now used in a slightly less derogatory way, to mean a nobody.

JERRY; 1. (CSR) wide awake or shrewd. A complicated bit of slang: Jerry-cum-mumble = tumble = understand. Probably obsolete since the Second World War **2.** water closet **3.** (early 19c) a chamber pot. Now rare but not obsolete in the north of England. One old music-hall routine linked jury, jerry and Bury in 'I'm sitting on the jerry,' 'No you're sitting on the jury'.

'But I come from Bury.' etc **4.** German **5.** a small and easily concealed pistol.

JERRY-BUILT; badly made, ie the way Germans did things.

JESSIE; (UK) homosexual, particularly in Glasgow.

JEWISH LIGHTNING; arson.

JEWISH PIANO; a cash register.

JIGGLERS; skeleton keys.

JIG-JIG; sexual intercourse. Common in Nigeria where bar girls dressed in white, spill over into the car park and, seizing potential punters by the testicles will ask 'You jig-jig?'

JILL OFF; (US) female, particularly lesbian, masturbation.

JILTER; (UK) a hotel thief. Certainly not in common usage but listed by Fabian in 1970 in *The Anatomy of Crime* (see bibliog.).

JIMMIES, to have the; (RS) diarrhoea. Jimmy Britts = shits. Originally Australian from the British boxer Jimmy Britts who fought there in the early years of this century.

JIMMY; 1. (CRS) to urinate. Jimmy riddle = piddle. The gap between the magistracy and the defendants was illustrated in the committal proceedings of a prison riot when, well into the afternoon one of the defendants put up his hand and when the magistrate asked what he wanted replied, to his confusion, 'Can I go and have a jimmy, sir?' **2.** (Can) an injection of narcotic **3.** (US) to open a safe with a jemmy or small crowbar. This is more usually called *jemmying* in England but *to jimmy open a safe* is used **4.** to obtain entry to cinemas, dog, race-tracks without payment.

JIMMY HIX; (CRS) a fix of drugs.

JIMS; the mackintosh brigade of men who watch prostitutes at work on the streets without actually engaging them. A milder version of the behaviour is those men who spend their lunch-hour watching women play netball.

JIMSCREECH; (UK) to obtain entry into a flat or house by conning the owner, as in 'I jimscreeched me way in.' First heard in London's Willesden area in the late 1980s, this is an example of language creation. It would appear to have its roots in the use of the word jimmy (qv) to obtain free entry.

JIVE; 1. (US) marijuana **2.** to kid, mostly used in London, and by the 1950s said to be obsolete. It is, however, a word common amongst West Indians. 'Don't jive me' has come to mean 'Don't mess me around', giving it a slightly more sinister interpretation **3.** sexual intercourse.

JOB; (UK) **1.** criminal act **2.** (19c) to convict or arrest. The police refer to their profession as 'the job' which is also the title of one of their specialist magazines.

JOB, on the; (UK) **1.** committing a criminal act **2.** having sexual intercourse.

JOCK; (US) a jockey.

JOCKER; (US 19–20c) a young hobo in the power of an older, usually homosexual one. The children's song, 'The Big Rock Candy Mountain' is really a siren song from 'a burly bum' to a young man, offering such delights as lemonade springs, hens laying soft-boiled eggs, bulldogs with rubber teeth and cops with wooden legs. As Kenneth Allsop remarks in *Hard Travelling*, had the BBC understood the lyrics it is doubtful that they would have played the Burl Ives record with such enthusiasm so many Saturday mornings on 'Children's Favourites'.

JOCKETTE; (US) a female jockey.

JOCKEY; 1. a prostitute's client **2.** a contraceptive sheath. A term used by the girls in a derisory manner.

JOCK OFF; (UK) to substitute an unfashionable jockey, particularly one who is the horse's usual rider, for a stronger or more fashionable one for a big race. (A prime exponent of getting rides on fancied horses was Lester Piggott.) This occurs much more frequently in flat racing than in national hunt racing, mainly because the stallion fees for the winner of a classic or other group race will be so much greater. It is also done if the stable wishes to land a betting coup.

JOE; a gun.

JOE GHIRR; (CRS) prison. Joe Ghirr = stir, so-called because porridge, the staple diet

of prisoners, had to be stirred. It is doubtful if it is in use today but Fabian (see bibliog.) lists it as current as late as 1955.

JOEY; (UK) **1.** a parcel illegally sent out of prison **2.** (1980s) a young person bullied by an older youth into stealing or mugging on his behalf. **3.** (US) a person who takes the place at home of a person serving a prison sentence. A situation likely to lead to all sorts of problems including a Dear John (qv) letter.

JOEYING; stealing from handbags.

JOHN; (UK) **1.** a penis and therefore **2.** a prostitute's client **3.** an unknown person. John Doe was a legal fiction for the purposes of bringing certain actions in the courts of the 19c **4.** an older homosexual protecting a younger one **5.** (US) the lavatory. From the old euphemism 'I'm going to see cousin John' **6.** a contraceptive sheath. See also *jockey*.

JOHN LAW; a police officer, usually a senior one.

JOHNNIE; (UK) condom or contraceptive sheath.

JOHN THOMAS; (UK) the penis. Originally an upper-class euphemism, popularised by Mellors in DH Lawrence's *Lady Chatterley's Lover*.

JOHNSON; (UK) a prostitute's bully. Again no longer common but listed by Fabian (see bibliog.). In America the word meant a tramp or drifter.

JOINT; 1. (US) marijuana cigarette **2.** penis **3.** cheap nightclub.

JOLLY BEANS; (US) Benzedrine. The Metropolitan Police keep an up-to-date list of terms used by drug abusers. This featured on a 1960s list, as did joy pop (qv).

JOLT; (US) to sentence to imprisonment.

JOY POP; (UK) a now-and-then injection.

JOY TRAIL; the vagina.

JUDY; a prostitute.

JUG; 1. (US) a bank **2.** (UK) a prison. This probably derives from either the Scots *joug* = the pillory, or the French *joug* = a yoke **3.** to imprison.

JUGS; (US) breasts.

JUG UP; (Can) prison meal.

JUICE; the current in the electric chair.

JUMP; 1. (UK) to jump out and attack. See also **mug**. Scots mainly Glasgow (and also UKbl) **2.** to escape (see also *jumping China*) **3.** (UKbl) to arrest.

JUMPER; (UK) **1.** a thief who steals particularly from offices. See also *stair jumper* **2.** a ticket inspector who joins a train when it is in motion.

JUMPING CHINA; (UK) a partner in an escape. (The China is his mate from the rhyming slang China plate = mate.)

JUMP UP; (UK) to steal from the back of parked lorries. The theft was accomplished by jumping up on to the tailboard. The Metropolitan Police came in for some criticism when, early in 1988, they left a lorry laden with goodies in the West End as a trap for thieves. The tailboard was left down and problems arose when a uniformed constable, not in the know, kept passing and putting the tailboard back in place 2. sexual intercourse. (Another example of how the same expressions are used for both sexual and criminal behaviour.)

JUMP UP MERCHANT; 1. a thief of goods from the backs of lorries 2. a young

upwardly mobile criminal. See also buck.

JUNK; (US) narcotics.

JUNKER or **JUNKIE;** (US) one addicted to narcotics.

JUNKYARD DOG; (US) an evil-tempered or vicious person. From the dogs used to guard junkyards. A black wrestler has made a career for himself under the name of The Junk Yard Dog. Curiously he is usually the blue eyes (qv) and is a great favourite with the children in the audience, a sort of American Big Daddy. The name is derived from the American expression 'Mad as a junkyard dog'.

KAKER; (Yiddish) excrement and so anything unpleasant.

KANGAROO; 1.(US) pimp **2.** (US) prison tobacco, from rhyming slang: kangaroo = chew **3.** (RS) a prison warder, from rhyming slang: kangaroo = screw **4.** (UK 19c) rhyming slang for Jew. Often reduced to kanger. Now rare in this context.

KANGAROO COURT; (Can) prison disciplinary board. The origins of the phrase do not appear to have any connection with Australia. A kangaroo at the turn of the century was either an unjust sentence of imprisonment or a mock trial held by inmates when another prisoner was dealt with for an offence such as child molestation – something which still happens today. The point is undoubtedly that the whole procedure is manifestly unfair – and the implication is that so is that of the disciplinary board.

KARFLICK; (Glas) pronunciation of Catholic. Term of abuse used by Protestant youths from late 1960s.

KARZI; see *Carsi*.

KEEP CAVVY; (UK) to keep look-out. Current in south London. It is a corruption of the old schoolboy tag 'cave', and is originally from the Latin meaning beware as in *cave canem* found on surburban gates where there is a dog. The schoolboy use is said to have originated at Eton in the 19c but it was common in all public schools. It is an interesting example of the belief that if a foreign or strange language is used no one will understand the speaker except those in the know. Clearly it was not thought by the boys that their masters had even a rudimentary knowledge of Latin.

KEEP DIXIE; (UK)
Liverpudlian word for keeping
look-out. Used only on the
Everton side of the Mersey
River. Dixie Dean was one of the
most popular footballers to play
for the club.

KEEP DOG; (UK) to keep a
look-out. Used in London and
often by three-card tricksters of
whom the look out man is called
the dog eye.

KEEP NIX; (Liverpool)
keeping look-out.

KEEP SIX; (Can) prison term
for keeping look-out.

KEISTER; 1. (US 19c)
handbag, small safe **2.** (US 20c)
buttocks **3.** (US 19c) a
pickpocket's term for the rear
trouser pocket. Chapman (see
bibliog.) suggests that the use of
the word meaning buttocks may
be from the British word kist or
chest or the German *kiste*
transferred to the buttocks, a
place of concealment, and so
relating back to **1.** by way of the

pickpocket's language. Certainly
the rectum has always been a
place where valuables could be
concealed – as in the present-day
practice of smuggling drugs in
the anus.

KEISTER SHAFTING;
(US) anal intercourse.

KEN; (UK) lodging house
(chiefly a Gypsy term).

KETTLE; (UK) a watch.

KHYBER; (RS) the buttocks,
'He needs a good kick up the
Khyber.' Khyber Pass = arse.

KIBBITZER; (US) from the
Yiddish. A watcher at a card or
other game. Particularly one who
gives unsought advice.

KICK; (US) **1.** a pocket. Used
mainly by gamblers, as in 'He
put the bank-roll in his kick'.
Refer Scarne (see bibliog.) **2.**
excitement, thrill, as in 'I get a
kick out of you.'

KICK ASS; (US) to behave
roughly to inferiors. Particularly
used in respect of police officers
to minority groups.

KICK, GOING ON A; (UK)
an intensive period of drug
taking.

KICK THE BUCKET; to
die. From the practice of
standing on a bucket, to put the

noose around one's neck and then kicking the bucket away to commit suicide.

KICK THE HABIT; to break a narcotic habit. So called because after a fairly mild first 48 hours of withdrawal the user begins to sweat, develop chills and experience muscle spasms and kicking movements.

KID; (US 19c) a gunman as well as a person of extreme youth. All the western films had 'Kids' in them. In real life William Bonney was Billy the Kid, and Harry Longbaugh was The Sundance Kid who rode with Butch Cassidy (possibly aka William Phelps).

KIDDY PORN; (US and UK) magazines and films containing pictures of children in the sexual act.

KIFE; 1. (US) to swindle, from circus and carnival slang **2.** to steal **3.** (UK) a bed.

KIFERING; (US) swindling, stealing **2.** the act of sexual intercourse.

KIKE; derogatory term for a Jewish person. When the immigrants of the 19c landed at Ellis Island, New York, many could not write their names. They would not make a cross as their mark and instead drew a circle. When asked what that was they would reply 'Kikel'.

KILLING; (US and UK) **1.** a very large profit made in a very short time. Often used of a successful gamble on stock or commodity markets **2.** (UKbl) mass robbery and fight.

KILO; (UK) a large amount of drugs, not necessarily that exact weight.

KING BUNG; (US) **1.** a white slaver **2.** a brothel keeper.

KINKY; 1. (UK and US) of unnatural sexual habits. In the film *PJ/New Face in Hell*, Gayle Hunnicutt, asked why she stays with Raymond Burr replies 'He would have to be a lot uglier and kinkier for this little girl to trade in her nightie' **2.** stolen goods (now obsolete) **3.** to be kinky of; to be suspicious of, to dislike **4.** crooked or unfair.

KIP; (UK) **1.** a bed, lodging house and so **2.** to sleep.

Originally used by tramps and now in common usage.

KIPPER; (Can and Aus) an Englishman. Two-faced, yellow-bellied and no guts.

KIRKBUZZER; (US 19c) a pickpocket who worked in churches during services. A Chicago gang was persuaded to give up this line of work in return for the promise of the rights to the World's Fair 1893. It is said that some urban churches at the turn of the century displayed notices 'Beware of pickpockets'.

KITE; 1. (UK early 19c) now a cheque, but originally a worthless bill of exchange **2.** (US 20c) a letter or note often one smuggled into or out of prison.

KITE, to fly a; (US) to smuggle a letter out of prison.

KIT HAS COME; (UK 19–20c) monthly period has arrived.

KITING; (UK) passing worthless or stolen cheques. See also *kite*. Now a very popular crime as credit cards have become so common. The groundwork is done, usually, by young girls, often with no previous convictions, in the almost certain knowledge that even if they are caught they will not receive an immediate prison sentence. The going rate in England in 1988 for a complete stolen cheque book and back-up banker's card was £150.

KNEE BENDER; a churchgoer or self-righteous person.

KNEECAPPING; shooting or drilling a hole in the kneecap of an informer. The effect is both to cripple the victim and to serve as a warning to others. Introduced by the IRA in Northern Ireland.

KNEE TREMBLE; sexual intercourse in the standing position. It is erroneously believed that this method acts as a contraceptive.

KNOB; (UK) **1.** penis. See also *nob* **2.** the head.

KNOBBER; (US 20c) male homosexual transvestite prostitute. Chapman suggests this may be either because of the false nipples they wear or because they give 'knob jobs'.

KNOBS; (US 20c) breasts.

KNOCK; 1. (UK and US) to make disparaging remarks: 'Don't knock the rock' **2.** to cheat or fail to pay a debt **3.** (UK 16c) to have intercourse **4.** (UK) to steal; common amongst Glasgow youth gangs of the late 1960s.

KNOCKBACK; the refusal of parole to a prisoner.

KNOCK DOWN GINGER; the children's game of ringing doorbells and then running away.

KNOCKERS; 1. (US 19c) The fist **2.** (US) a drug addict trying to break the habit **3.** (UK 19c) someone who fails to pay a debt **4.** (US) to cop a knocker, to be arrested. Mainly used by tramps **5.** a person who continually makes disparaging remarks **6.** breasts **7.** testicles.

KNOCKER, on the; speculative visits to houses and flats to buy antiques, often from elderly ladies who can be frightened and deceived into selling their goods at far less than their true worth.

KNOCKINGS; (UK) a recent term for the closing speeches at a criminal trial, ie when you 'knock' the other side's case, making derisive and disparaging remarks about the evidence.

KNOCKING SHOP; (UK mid-19c) brothel, whorehouse.

KNOCK OFF; 1. (UK 20c) to steal **2.** (US 20c) to murder **3.** (US 20c) to arrest.

KNOCK OUT; 1. (UK 20c) dispose cheaply of stolen goods, often quite openly in a shop used as the front (qv) for a long firm (qv) **2.** (US 20c) beautiful woman, as in 'She's a knock out' from the boxing term.

KNOCK OVER, to; to rob.

KNOCK UP, to; (US) to make pregnant.

KNUCKLE SANDWICH; a hard blow, especially in the mouth.

KOSHER; honest, not stolen. From the Yiddish. It also means to be trustworthy (from the same derivation).

KOTCHEL; money. At one time cotchel (sic) was a term for bundle, which of course included money. This use is extremely rare. More lately the term was used in and around Dewsbury, Yorkshire in the early- to mid-1980s. Kotchel could be blue (five pounds) or brown (ten pounds. There are signs the word is acquiring countrywide appeal.

KREMLIN; New Scotland Yard.

KURVA; a prostitute, from the Yiddish.

L

LAG; prisoner.

LAGGED; sentenced.

LAGGING; prison sentence of more than three years.

LAG, OLD; recidivist.

LAJARAS; (US) Hispanic name for police, probably deriving from an officer named O'Hara.

LAM, on the; on the run.

LAME, to come up; to be unable to pay gambling debts.

LAME BRAIN; a stupid person.

LAMP, to; 1. to see, to look **2.** to hit in the face.

LAMPING; shining lights into the eyes of rabbits or other game whilst poaching at night.

LAMPS; 1. eyes **2.** spectacles.

LARRIKIN; (Aus) a hoodlum.

LASH; (Aus) a trick or swindle.

LASHED UP; 1. burdened with somebody **2.** possibly being married but more likely to be involved in a temporary relationship. See also *shacked up*.

LASHING; (UKbl) a violent robbery.

LAST MILE; euphemism for the walk from the condemned cell to the gallows. In practice in the United Kingdom it was an extremely short walk.

LAUNDER, to; to change stolen money at a discount. In less sophisticated times this was done at race-tracks, in gambling clubs and from time to time with the assistance of a dishonest solicitor. Now laundering has become an international business. It is, however, still possible to find instances of stolen money which has been marked by a bank cashier (and so is identifiable) put through the doors of charity shops. The charity shops then bank the notes, which are thus untraceable back to the thief. This altruism is however rare. Marked money is usually burned.

LAW, JOHN; see *John Law*.

LAY; a woman considered only in sexual terms, as in 'She's a good lay.'

LAY, to; to have sexual intercourse.

LAY DOWN; a remand in custody.

LAY HIM DOWN, to; to kill.

LAY ON THE HIP; to smoke opium. From the comfortable position assumed.

LAY PAPER, to; to pass worthless cheques.

LEAD IN YOUR PENCIL, to have; to have an erection or to be capable of sexual intercourse.

LEATHER; 1. the anus **2.** wallet or purse.

LEERY, to be; 1. to be wary or cautious **2.** to be bad-tempered or disagreeable.

LEGGNER; a one-year prison sentence.

LEG IT; to run away.

LEGIT; honest, straight, not stolen.

LEG OVER, to have a; to have sexual intercourse.

LEGSHAKE ARTIST; (Aus) a pickpocket.

LEG UP DEFENCE; a defence which needs the active co-operation of the solicitor in constructing it. For example: 'Do you need a leg up brief?' = 'Do you need a solicitor who will fabricate a defence?'

LETTUCE; paper money.

LEVEL, on the; honest, straight.

LEVEL, to; to admit or confess.

LEZ(ZIE); abbreviation of lesbian, as in 'Is she a lez?'

LF; see *long firm*.

LIBERTY; an unfair advantage taken of someone, usually the speaker. More serious is *a right liberty* and, when the doer is totally out of order (qv), the advantage taken is a *diabolical liberty*.

LICK; 1. a blow **2.** style.

LIFE, the; pimping, as in 'What's Tommy do?' 'The life.'

LIFER; 1. a prisoner sentenced to life imprisonment **2.** a prison officer, a term used by them to describe themselves.

LIFT, the; stealing from shops.

LIGGER; someone who gets into parties, premières, launches uninvited.

LILY; a male homosexual.

LIMIT, to go the; to have sexual intercourse. A term used mainly by adolescents to describe how they have progressed on a previous date or to assess another's chances, as in 'You might get a handful of sprats but she won't go the limit.'

LIMP WRIST; an effeminate person, a homosexual.

LINE, on the; (Aus) under police observation.

LINEN; (RS) a newspaper. Linen draper = paper.

LINER; (UKbl) policeman, particularly a member of the pickpocket squad.

LINE UP; (US) identification parade.

LIQUID LAUGHTER; (Aus) vomiting.

LITTLE MAN IN A BOAT; clitoris, from the believed resemblance.

LIVERPOOL KISS; a hit on the mouth.

LIVERPOOL LEG; to urinate in someone's pocket. Said to have originated at football matches when, because of the lack of lavatory facilities, a supporter on the packed terraces would relieve himself in his neighbour's trouser or jacket pocket.

LIVIN; (UKbl) person.

LIVIN DRUM, to do a; (UKbl) a burglary.

LOADED; full of **1.** drink **2.** money **3.** drugs.

LOAN SHARK; money lender at extortionate terms, usually 'six for five' – five pounds borrowed must be repaid at six pounds the next week.

LOCUST; a policeman's club, because the heaviest clubs were made from locust wood.

LOID; (RS) celluloid. See also Harold.

LOLLY; money.

LOLLIPOP, to; (RS) to inform. Lollypop = shop.

LONG FIRM; a dishonest business where goods are bought on credit and then sold at a substantial discount. The vendors are never paid and only the front (qv) is left to face the wrath of the creditors and court.

LONG GREEN; paper money.

LONG ONE; £100, sometimes a £1000.

LONG ROD; a rifle.

LOOGAN; a gunman.

LOON; (Aus) a pimp.

LOOPJOINT; an arcade of machines which show sex films on a continuous loop. Coins are fed into a slot and the aim of the arcade manager is to set the machine to ensure the money runs out just before a crucial part of the action and so forcing the punter to invest again. They are only really an adult and more expensive version of the 'What the butler saw' penny machines on the pier.

LOSE ONE'S OLLIE, to; to lose control totally, from Oliver Hardy's behaviour towards Stan Laurel.

LOOT; money or goods, often illegally obtained. From the Urdu.

LUDE; Quaalude, a depressant drug.

LUG; ear, originally Scots.

LUMBER; 1. (Scots) a girl taken home after a dance **2.** spectators in a casino.

LUMBER, to; to take advantage of someone's kindness.

LUMP; cannabis.

LUMP, the; earnings at a building site for which tax is avoided.

LUMPY JUMPER; (Army) a female.

LURK, to; (Navy) to impose on someone's kindness.

LUSH; a drunk. Lushington's was a 19c London Brewery.

LUSH ROLLER; someone, often a pickpocket, who

specialises in stealing from drunks.

LUSH UP; to stand a drink.

LYNCHING; an informal hanging, probably named after Captain William Lynch who set out to remove the unruly element from Pittsylvania County in Virginia. Another claimant for the eponym is Charles Lynch who with his brother founded Lynchburg, also in Virginia. The first lynching seems to have taken place in September 1780.

M

M; 1. morphine 2. marijuana.

MACE, to; 1. to get something for nothing 2. to throw spice in the eyes of a victim during a robbery 3. to steal or cheat.

MACK; a pimp, often black.

MADAM; a female brothel keeper.

MADAM, to; 1. to tell lies; from the rhyming slang Madam de Luce = spruce (fib) 2. to spin a tale, to flatter, as in 'Don't madam me.'

MAGAZINE; 1. a six-month prison sentence. From the time it would take a person with little education to read a book 2. (US) a 60-day sentence. Presumably they read more quickly over there.

MAGDALENE; a reformed prostitute, from the biblical connotation.

MAGGOT; (USbl) a white person.

MAGSMAN; now a petty thief but originally a well-dressed swindler.

MAINLINE, to; to inject drugs into the vein.

MAJOON; candy, similar to Turkish delight, eaten for its psychedelic qualities. Also known as *ma'jun*.

MAKE, to; 1. to achieve sexual intercourse 2. to steal or rob 3. to recognise.

MAMA BEAR; (US) a policewoman.

MANOR; district marked out by the police, as in 'I'm not having thieving on my manor.' See also turf.

MAP; the face.

MAQ; abbreviation of the French *maquereau* = mackerel, a pimp or low-life character. See also *mec*.

MARACAS; the breasts.

MARATHON; a long evening date for a call girl, which will involve dinner and dancing before going to bed with the client.

MARBLE ORCHARD; a cemetery.

MARK; the victim of a confidence trick.

MARKER; 1. a signed promissory note **2.** a favour done in the expectation that another will be done in return.

MARK POINTS, to; to keep watch in order to assess the suitability of a situation for theft or robbery.

MARY; 1. lesbian **2.** passive homosexual, a particularly common name given by homosexuals to themselves **3.** morphine.

MARY JANE; marijuana.

MATCH BOX; enough marijuana to make about six cigarettes.

MAUI-WAUI; (pronounced mau-wee wau-wee) Hawaiian-grown marijuana.

MAYTAG; (US) prison term for weak male unable to protect himself from homosexual rape.

MAYTAG, to; to commit the act of homosexual rape.

MAZUMA, the old; money, from the Hebrew word for money.

MEAL TICKET; a person on whom another depends for his or her livelihood. Originally a boxer's manager.

MEAT; the penis.

MEAT, to beat the; to masturbate.

MEAT EATER; 1. a police officer who will actively seek bribes **2.** a prostitute who will perform fellatio.

MEAT RACK; place, eg London's Piccadilly Circus station, where homosexuals go to select young male prostitutes.

MEAT SALESMAN; pimp.

MEAT WAGON; police van used to take in prostitutes.

MEC; pimp. See also *maq*.

MECHANIC; 1. an expert card player, usually a dishonest one **2.** a hired killer.

MECHANIC'S GRIP; a way of holding a deck of cards with three fingers curled around the long edge and the index finger at the narrow upper edge further from the body.

MEET, a; a meeting arranged by a criminal's confidant either with a police officer or an intermediary to discuss terms of bail, and what evidence will be given at a trial. In this connotation it almost always involves or leads to the passing of money and is essentially a corrupt rendezvous. It can also apply to a meeting with an informer when again money is likely to pass.

MELLOW OFF; to quieten down, as in 'I told him to mellow off'.

MERKIN; A pubic wig. Originally worn by sufferers of venereal disease. Later it was a term used for hair dye. In the film *Dr Strangelove* the American president was named Merkin Muffley.

MESHUGGER; (Yiddish) mad, but often used as a term of endearment.

MET, the; the Metropolitan Police.

METER MAID; female traffic warden. See also *Dickless Tracey*.

METHODIST; a two-headed axe used in a lumber camp.

MEXICAN BROWN; a superior type of marijuana.

MEZZROLE; a highly potent marijuana cigarette resembling those once sold by jazz clarinettist Mezz Mezzrow.

MIDGE'S DICK; something very small.

MIGHTY MEZZ; outsize marijuana cigarette. See also *mezzrole*.

MIN; 1. policeman or woman **2.** abbreviation of minge (qv).

MINCE PIES, MINCIES; (RS) eyes.

MING; north London slang for

the police. Ming was the evil opponent of Dan Dare in the *Eagle* comic.

MINGE; the vagina.

MING ON THE WING; look-out cry: the police are coming.

MIRACULOUS; very drunk. The implication is 'It's miraculous he's still alive.'

MISS; to miss the vein when injecting.

MISSIONARY POSITION; common position of intercourse with the man lying on top of the woman. So called because the missionaries tried to persuade their converts only to have coitus that way.

MITT; the hand.

MITT, to; (US) **1.** to shake hands **2.** to arrest.

MITT CAMP; (US) a fortune teller's booth or tent.

MITTS; (US) handcuffs.

MIXER; a person who deliberately causes trouble.

M.O.; *modus operandi*, the way in which a criminal regularly commits his crimes.

MOB, the; the navy.

MOCKERS; evil fortune or the evil eye as in 'He's put the mockers on me.' Originally the word meant depression or 'the blues'.

MODPLOD; Ministry of Defence policeman.

MOGGIES; amphetamines.

MOLL; 1. (Aus) prostitute **2.** a girlfriend or sweetheart but often used for a girl who hangs around with criminals eg 'a gangster's moll'.

MOLL BUZZER; a thief who steals from women.

MOMSER; (Yiddish) literally a bastard, generally an unspecific term of abuse for someone disliked by the speaker.

MONDAY BOY or **GIRL;** a thief who steals from clotheslines; derisory name for a petty criminal. Before the arrival of the launderette and the washing machine, Monday was the traditional washday.

MONEY BOX; the vagina. Children's usage from the shape.

MONEYMAKER; the vagina.

MONKEY; (UK and US) £500 or $500.

MONKEY ON ONE'S BACK; to have a narcotic addiction.

MONKEY'S, not to give a; not to care, as in 'I don't give a monkey's.'

MONNICKER; nickname.

MOOCH, to; to beg or obtain free goods and services. See also *mump.*

MOODY; dishonest, stolen, lies.

MOODY, to do a; to behave in a way not approved of by the police, eg a rejection in court of a written confession, an unexpected plea of not guilty, as in 'He's gone and done a moody.' From the rhyming slang Moody and Sankey = hanky panky. Moody and Sankey were American evangelists in the late 19c.

MOODY BOB; the police.

MOOLA(H); (early 20c) money.

MOON; one month's imprisonment.

MOON, to; to expose one's bare buttocks.

MOONER; a psychopathic criminal, one who commits crimes such as rape for no profit. From the belief that such people are affected by the full moon.

MOONING; the act of exposing. It has had a particular vogue at football matches. In the spring of 1988 a number of the Wimbledon players mooned at a match after their English FA Cup Final triumph.

MOONLIGHT, to; to take a second job, the earnings from which are not declared for tax.

MOONLIGHTER; (USbl) a prostitute.

MOONLIGHT FLIT, to do a; to leave a tenancy without paying the back rent.

MOONSHINE; 1. illicit whisky **2.** lies.

MULE

MOOR, the; Dartmoor prison.

MORGUEY MANOR; a well policed district and therefore one dangerous for house-breakers.

MORNING GLORY; horse which shows great promise on the training gallops but cannot repeat the form on a race-track.

MOTHER; a drug pusher, especially a homosexual one.

MOTHER FUCKER; self-explanatory term of abuse, mainly of black usage.

MOUNTAIN DEW; illegal whisky.

MOUNTAIN OYSTERS; calves', or less commonly sheeps' testicles. Often deep fried and eaten with a chilli sauce.

MOUSE; 1. a bruise near the eye caused by a blow **2.** a homosexual.

MOUSE'S EAR; the vagina. From the expression 'Tight as a mouse's ear.'

MOUTH MUSIC; cunnilingus.

MOUTHPIECE; a criminal lawyer, especially a barrister.

MUCKER; a friend or mate.

MUFF DIVING; cunnilingus.

MUG; 1. the face **2.** fool, used as a term of derision by prostitutes of their clients.

MUG, to; 1. to take identification photographs for police records **2.** to rob. The word seems to have been first used in Canal Street, Buffalo New York, and the practice was the quickest and easiest way of obtaining money to buy another mug of beer.

MUGGLE; marijuana.

MUG PUNTER; a foolish gambler, eg one who is attracted by the odds of 500–1 laid against a horse known to be in a race solely as a pacemaker.

MULE; person used by drug traders to carry the drugs across borders.

MUMP; to beg or, as a policeman, to eat and obtain goods free from restaurants, cafés and shops in return either for some protection or for turning a blind eye to after hours drinking.

MUPPET; 1. a uniformed policeman **2.** a lay magistrate. See also *woodentop*.

MURPHY GAME, the; 1. beating and robbing of a prostitute's client **2.** a confidence trick such as corner game (qv). So named because of the alleged simplicity of the Irish.

MUSCLE; a man hired as a physical protector; a strong-arm man.

MUSH; 1. the mouth **2.** (Liverpool) prostitute's client **3.** friend or mate. In this case the word is pronounced with a short 'u'.

MUTTON; deaf. Probably a contraction of the rhyming slang Mutt and Jeff = deaf.

MUTTON DRESSED AS LAMB; a middle-aged or elderly woman wearing clothes more suitable for a young girl.

MYSTERY; 1. a girl, specifically a virgin, as in 'It's a mystery how she's still a virgin.' Another version is that a mystery is a strange girl, possibly a runaway, hanging around in London's West End **2.** (US police) a crime difficult if not impossible to solve.

NAB; (B1) a policeman.

NAB, to; to arrest.

NAG; a useless racehorse.

NAIL; a cigarette. Abbreviation of coffin nail (qv).

NAIL, to; 1. to obtain sufficient evidence to secure a conviction, to arrest **2.** to steal.

NANCY; the buttocks.

NANCY BOY; effete homosexual.

NARK; police informer, also known as *copper's nark*.

NARK IT; order to stop a particular activity, to be quiet.

NARNA; a fool, as in 'A proper narna'. Abbreviation of banana.

NASH, to; to run away. Warning shout that a crime is being interrupted.

NATURAL; in dice the first throw of 7 or 11 which is automatically a winning throw.

NAUTCH; the vagina.

NEBBISH; (Yiddish) a total loser.

NECKTIE; the hangman's noose.

NEDDY; a cosh.

NEEDLE; 1. hypodermic syringe **2.** bad feeling, rivalry, anger.

NEEDLE MATCH; boxing or other sporting contest where there is real or feigned bad feeling between the contestants. Very useful in the sale of tickets to punters who are led to believe they will be getting something extra for their money.

NETTIE; an outside lavatory. Possibly a contraction of 'the necessary'.

NEVES; (back slang) seven-year sentence.

NEWINGTON BUTTS; the stomach. Rhyming slang = guts.

N.F.A.; no fixed abode; a reason for not giving a defendant bail.

NICK; police station.

NICK, in good; in good shape or condition.

NICK, to; 1. to arrest **2.** to steal. A possible origin of the word is from the nick-pot, an 18c beer mug which had a false bottom so the customer received less than he paid for. He was caught or nicked. A suggestion in *Police Review* in 1960 was that it had connotions with Old Nick, the devil.

NIFTY; 1. £50 **2.** insolent, cocky.

NIFTY, a bit of; sexual intercourse.

NIGERIAN LAGER; Guinness.

NIGGER MINSTREL; Durophet capsule.

NIGHTHAWK; burglar.

NIPPERS; 1. handcuffs **2.** small children.

NIX; nothing. From the German *nichts*.

NOB; 1. penis **2.** member of upper strata of society **3.** the knave in a suit of cards.

NOBBINS; coins thrown into a boxing ring in appreciation of a good bout; traditionally the proceeds are shared equally between the boxers although often the winner will give the loser his share.

NOBBLE, to; to get at either by injury, threats or bribery. Horses, greyhounds and juries are particularly common targets.

NOD, on the; 1. drowsy state following an injection of narcotics **2.** a very close finish in a horse race, literally the horse which nods its head on the line.

NOD, the; the referee's decision.

NODDING AND SMILING; the act of soliciting males in a public lavatory.

NODDY; a policeman, after the character by Enid Blyton.

NODDY BIKE; a police motor cycle.

NO FT; reply by suspect, meaning no comment, when interviewed by police; based on the advertising campaign by the *Financial Times* 'No FT, no comment'.

NOISE; heroin.

NONCE; child molester.

NONCING; 1. passing stolen cheques. This was an expression in use in the home counties in the 1960s but seems never to have been used more widely. **2.** child molestation. This is a southern expression.

NO NECK; an idiot.

NOOKIE; sexual intercourse.

NOSE; 1. a police informer **2.** a detective

NOSE BAG, to; to eat.

NOSE CANDY; cocaine, because it is taken through the nose.

NOSH; 1. food **2.** to steal selectively.

NOSH ROD; (Army) a fork.

NO SHOW; a person who fails to claim or cancel his reservation on an air flight. Lately in use by restaurateurs for customers who book tables and then do not appear.

NU; (Yiddish) so what? A derisory comment showing indifference, as in 'I've got stomach ache.' 'Nu.' 'What do you want me to do about it?' See also *tough titty*.

NUDNIK; (Yiddish) a fool or loser.

NUMBER, to have someone's; to know some secret about a person's past or behaviour and thereby be able to exert some influence over them.

NUMBERS RACKET; illegal American but originally English lottery run rather on the lines of the football pools, based on daily horse racing results. The true odds against winning are 1000–1 but the punter is only paid at 600–1. It is said that over

20 million people play the numbers game annually. The turnover runs into billions in America.

NUT; 1. the expenses incurred by thieves whilst setting up and carrying out a theft or robbery **2.** a bribe given to a public official **3.** the principal sum loaned by a loan shark. See also *vig* **4.** the head.

NUT, to; to use one's head in a fight.

NUT AND GUT REPORTS; mental and medical reports requested by the court to determine the fitness of the defendant either to plead to the charge or undergo a period of imprisonment.

NUT HOUSE; mental hospital.

NUTS; the testicles.

NUTTER; madman, mentally unstable person.

NYMPHO; term of abuse used of a girl who offers sexual favours readily, even if she does not qualify for the medical definition of nymphomaniac.

O

O; opium.

OBBO; police observation on suspected criminals.

OCHRE; money, from the colour of gold.

O.D.; overdose of drugs.

ODD; the police, particularly detectives.

ODDLOT; a police car. In fashion at the height of the teddyboy era.

OFAY; black term of abuse for a white person. Possibly a corruption of foe.

OFFICE, to; to warn or tip somebody off.

OFF THE CUFF; impromptu, unrehearsed, free.

OILED; drunk.

OLD ARMY GAME; a swindle or trick.

OLD BILL; the police.

OLD LADY; 1. wife **2.** mother. There is a tendency for working class people and particularly the elderly male to call his wife 'mother'. The shortest will on record is one which said 'All to mother'. It resulted in a probate action when evidence was given that the testator regularly called his wife 'mother'.

OLD MAN; 1. husband **2.** father **3.** term of endearment for an old friend.

OLD SMOKEY; the electric chair.

OL' SPARKEY; nickname for the electric chair in Florida. When the mass murderer Ted Bundy was executed in January 1989 part of the waiting crowd sang 'On top of ol' Sparkey'.

ON A PROMISE; 1. awaiting money in the form of a bribe, reward for information. It may apply either to the police or to criminals. The promise is often not forthcoming **2.** on a date. The implication is that there is the promise of sex at the end of the evening.

ONCER; one pound.

ON DAB; to be on a police disciplinary charge.

ONE-EYED TROUSER SNAKE; (Aus) the penis.

ONNER; £100.

ON THE ARM; freeloading, particularly by the police. See also *mump* and *mooch*.

ON THE FLY; in a hurry.

ON THE GAME; prostitution.

ON THE JOB; 1. committing a crime **2.** having sexual intercourse.

ON THE KNOCK; knocking at homes to persuade, perhaps

by way of intimidation, old people to sell antiques and other valuables cheaply.

ON THE LAM; on the run from prison or the police.

ON THE PAD; wholesale bribery. Criminals pay a set fee to a police station or precinct which is then shared out between police officers according to rank and length of service.

ON YOUR TOD; see *tod*.

OPPO; 1. the opposition **2.** the opposite number on a ship and therefore a friend.

ORCHESTRA STALLS; testicles. Rhyming slang orchestra stalls = balls.

OSCAR; 1. a pistol **2.** (RS) cash. Oscar Asche = cash. Originally Australian use. Asche was a musical comedy star of the early part of the century. His most celebrated role was in *Chu Chin Chow*.

OUT, an; a potentially winning defence to a criminal charge possibly, but not necessarily, an alibi.

OUT OF ORDER; in the wrong, taking an unfair advantage or impolite behaviour generally, as in 'He was out of order so I gave him a smack.'

OUTSIDE, the; prison term for the outside world.

OUTSIDE MAN; the man standing guard outside a building to warn the thieves of any coming police. A look-out on a three-card trick (qv) team.

OUT TO LUNCH; 1. crazy **2.** totally in the wrong.

OUT WITH THE RAGS; a horse unfavoured in the betting, from rags used during menstruation being hung out on the washing line.

OVERS; proceeds of a crime not yet divided up.

OVER THE BLUE WALL; (US) confined in a hospital for the criminally insane.

OVER THE WALL, to go; escape from prison.

OXFORD SCHOLAR; (RS) dollar. In the days when there were four dollars to the pound, an Oxford was five shillings.

OYSTER; a society woman employed to wear stolen jewellery in the hope she will receive an offer from a fence, and will, because of her social position, remain unsuspected by the police.

P

PACK; heroin.

PACK RAT; a small time thief.

PAD; 1. flat or room; **2.** list of names. See also *on the pad* **3.** cell used for violent inmates.

PADMATE; a cell mate.

PAIR OF BINS; binoculars.

PAKI, the; a corner shop. Scots usage for any corner shop now, irrespective of the race of the owners but originating with the number of such shops owned by Asians. It is not used in Scotland as a slur, merely as a description. See also *tally, the*.

PALATIC; incapably drunk, a corruption of paralytic.

PALM OIL; a bribe.

PAN, to; 1. to beg (Abbreviation of *panhandle*. Originally because beggars held out tin cups or pans.) **2.** to denigrate **3.** to strike.

PANGY; (Romany) five pounds.

PANHANDLE, to; to beg. See *pan*.

PAN OUT, to; to turn out, as in 'I don't know how it'll pan out.' Probably from the mining days when pans were shaken to see if there were small nuggets of gold amongst the stones and shale scooped from river beds.

PAPER HANGER; passer of bad cheques or forged notes.

PASTEL; (USpol) an unmarked police car.

PAVEMENT ARTIST; (UK) robber who specialises in wages snatches from the vans delivering money to banks.

PAVEMENT PIZZA; vomit on the pavement.

PAVEMENT PRINCESS; prostitute.

PAY-OFF; 1. dividend sharing by criminals **2.** regular bribe paid to prison warders or police.

110

PAYOLA; bribery. One form was the payment by record companies to disc jockeys to promote their records on their radio shows.

PC HARD; the officer who will interrogate a suspect roughly, threatening him with violence to obtain a confession. If this treatment is not successful his colleague *PC Soft* will take over, sympathising with the man and offering him cigarettes.

PEACH; 1. to inform **2.** the anus.

PECKER; the penis.

PEDIGREE; criminal record.

PEELER; 1. policeman, now used almost only in Northern Ireland. From Sir Robert Peel, the founder of the modern police force in 1829 **2.** prison officers, a term used only in north country prisons.

PEN; prison, from the US penitentiary.

PENCIL; the penis. See also *lead in your pencil.*

PERCHER; 1. shoplifter **2.** an easy arrest or victim.

PERCY, to point p. at the porcelain; to urinate. Just one of a number of Australian idioms which have gained general currency in the United Kingdom through the Barry Humphries' character Bazza MacKenzie.

PERP; (US) perpetrator, police term for suspect.

PETER; 1. a safe, (US) chest or portmanteau **2.** a prison or police cell **3.** (US) the penis.

PETERMAN; safe-breaker.

PICCOLO PLAYER; the active homosexual in fellatio. It can also refer to a prostitute who prefers to service clients in this way rather than by way of straight sex.

PICK-UP; chance encounter for sexual purposes.

PICK-UP, to; to steal from unattended cars.

PIECE; 1. a firearm **2.** a woman.

PIE EATER; (Aus) small-time criminal.

PIERHEAD JUMP; the late boarding of a ship.

PIG; policeman. Not, as might be thought, a modern American term but 19c English. Towards the end of the century it was used almost exclusively for plain-clothes detectives. Now it is back as a general term of abuse.

PIG BROTHER; (USbl) an informer especially to white authorities.

PIGEON; 1. police informer **2.** mark, target, someone to be plucked.

PIGEON DROP; one of the simplest and most common versions of a confidence trick. It requires two people to work the scam. The first finds a wallet or bag, apparently filled with money. The victim watches the discovery and a third person, in reality, the second member of the con team, comes on the scene to claim his share of the loot. For the trick to be worked, as in most confidence tricks, it requires an element of dishonesty or greed in the victim. The first person will then say he has police connections and will check whether the money is stolen. The report comes back that the money is probably itself hot either in the form of tax avoided or, in America where the scam is the most common, gambling money. The 'police connection' or sometimes employer of the first man will have 'offered to hold' the money until the victim and the second man in the trick can produce an equal sum to ensure they will act in good faith and keep the secret. The third man can immediately produce his deposit and the victim and the first man go to get their stakes. When the victim pays over his share the two artists disappear. The trick is also worked by the apparent deposit of the money in a hotel safe or locker with the victim given the receipt. In fact he has received a second useless ticket. In a third version he may actually get to claim the bag which will contain newspaper.

PIGEON PIE; any form of pie served to prisoners in Strangeways gaol in Manchester,

England. So called because of a former governor who kept pigeons.

PIKER; small-time cheat.

PIKEY; gypsy, from their frequent use of turnpikes.

PILLOW BITER; passive homosexual.

PIMP; a man who lives off the immoral earnings of prostitutes.

PIMP DUST; cocaine.

PINCH, to; to arrest.

PINEAPPLE; a bomb.

PIPE, to; to look at or examine.

PISS ARTIST; a drunk or at the very least a habitually heavy drinker.

PISS IT OUT THE WINDOW; to waste money, as in 'All I did was piss it out the window'. Often said by criminals who have spent their share of the proceeds in night clubs and on drink instead of buying launderettes.

PIT; a bed.

PITCH; 1. site used by street vendors, three-card tricksters or prostitutes **2.** sales talk and therefore **3.** the propositioning of a woman, as in 'Any minute now he'll make a pitch.'

PITS, the; ugly, disgusting.

PLANT; cache of narcotics.

PLANT, to; to put stolen goods or drugs in a suspect's pocket or among his possessions and thereby falsely provide evidence against him.

PLANTING BEETS; (Aus) vomiting.

PLASTERED; (RS) drunk. There is an extremely complicated theory that this evolves as follows: plaster of Paris = Aris = Aristotle = bottle.

PLASTIC, on the; using stolen credit cards to defraud banks and businesses.

113

PLATER; 1. a woman who will practice oral intercourse. Used also of homosexual men **2.** a poor quality racehorse. One which will only run in selling plates, the winner of which is auctioned in public after the race.

PLAYER; a member of a team of confidence tricksters.

PLOD; a uniformed police constable, from the character created by Enid Blyton.

POCKET MAN; (US) trusted member of criminal team who will hold proceeds of crime before the share-out.

POET'S DAY; (Army) Piss off early tomorrow's Saturday. Another version of TGIF (Thank God it's Friday).

POKE, a; wallet.

POKE, to; to have sexual intercourse.

POKEY; prison.

POLIS; (Scots) police.

POLLO; illegal Mexican immigrant to the United States. From the Spanish for chicken, because the immigrants are to be plucked by bandits operating on the US-Mexican border.

PONCE; a man who lives off the immoral earnings of a prostitute, but originally only a man (usually young) who was kept by a woman. This was also the more common meaning in America in the 20c.

PONCE, to; to beg or borrow, as in 'Can I ponce a fag off of you?'

PONTOON; 21 months' (occasionally years') imprisonment. One judge at the old inner London quarter sessions was known as 'Pontoon Charlie'. After hearing the mitigation from the defendant's barrister he would begin the sentencing with words such as 'I have listened very carefully to everything Mr Smith has had to say on your behalf and I must say it has made a great impression on me. I am favourably impressed . . .' The accused thought a spot of probation would be awarded. 'You will go to prison for 21 months and had it not been for the mitigation I have heard it would have been a great deal longer. Take him down.'

PONY; £25, possibly from the one-time going rate to be paid for a small horse.

PONY, to have a; (RS) to defecate. Pony and trap = crap.

PONY UP; to pay.

POOF; a homosexual or effeminate person. This may go back to the First World War derision aimed at those who puffed cigarettes rather than smoking the manly pipe or cigar, something itself stuffed with sexual symbolism.

POON or **POONTANG;** the vagina, originally of a negress or mulatto but now more generally used. The expression probably originated in Louisiana with its French-speaking population and is a corruption of the French *putain* = prostitute.

POP A WINDOW, to; smash and grab.

POPPY LOVE; an elderly Jewish male.

PORK; 1. a corpse. From the appearance of a body resembling, in colour anyway, a side of pork **2.** the penis.

PORK, to; to have sexual intercourse.

PORK PACKER; a necrophiliac.

PORRIDGE; imprisonment. Porridge was a staple prison diet and it is a tradition that if a prisoner does not eat his final bowl on the morning of his release he will return.

PORTSMOUTH DEFENCE; the justification for the robbery of a homosexual by a sailor. The defendant was so outraged by being sexually approached by the victim that he was compelled to give him a beating to defend his honour. The problem with his defence was that it left unexplained why the sailor had taken the victim's watch as well as giving him a kicking. Nevertheless in less enlightened times it often worked well with a jury.

POUND; (US) five-year prison sentence.

POWDER, to take a; to run away.

PRAT; 1. the bottom **2.** the vagina. Used as a term of abuse.

PRICK; 1. the penis **2.** foolish, obnoxious person.

PRODUCER; the form HORT 1 issued by traffic police officers for the production of driving licence, insurance certificate at a named police station.

PROS, the; the prosecution.

PROSS (IE); prostitute.

YOUNG BUSTY FRENCH MODEL
PLEASE RING

PUFF; cannabis.

PULL, a; an arrest for questioning, usually followed by a release without charge.

PULL, to; 1. to arrest as above **2.** to ride a horse in such a way as to stop it winning **3.** to persuade a girl to have sexual intercourse, as in 'He can't half pull the birds.'

PUMP, the; the heart.

PUMP, to; to interrogate.

PUMPING IRON; weight-lifting.

PUNK; formerly a young homosexual, now more usually a young, ill-mannered upstart, coward, petty criminal.

PUPPIES; shoes. 'My puppies are barking' = 'My shoes are hurting.'

PUSHER; 1. vendor or distributor of drugs **2.** passer of counterfeit money.

PUSH UP, to be at; pickpocketing.

PUSS; the cat o'nine tails; a flogging. Withdrawn, as was the use of the birch for young offenders, as a sentencing option in 1948. It was made of nine knotted rawhide thongs attached to a handle. In the 20c the punishment was used in cases of violence and accompanied a

prison term eg six years and six strokes of the cat.

PUSSIES; furs and fur coats.

PUSSY; 1. at one time a prostitute who, for an extra fee, would allow herself to be whipped by the cat o'nine tails but now **2.** sexual intercourse in general and specifically the vagina.

PUSSY HOUND; (US) a man obsessed with sex.

PUSSY PELMET; an ultra-short mini skirt.

PUSSY POSSE; the Vice Squad.

PUSSY WHIPPED, to be; to be totally dominated by a woman and her use of sex.

PUT AWAY; sent to gaol.

PUT OUT, to; to make oneself available for sex, as in 'Does she put out?' Invariably unpaid.

PUT THE HORNS ON, to; 1. to cuckold **2.** to try to change one's luck in a casino by carrying a rabbit's foot, or by changing position at a table.

PUT YOUR HANDS UP, to; to confess to crime and to plead guilty.

Q

Q; 1. San Quentin prison **2.** abbreviation for queen, queer.

Q.E.; Queen's Evidence; evidence given by an accomplice against former members of a gang in return for a lighter sentence.

QT; quiet, secrecy, as in 'We did it on the qt.'

QUAIL; a young sexually attractive woman.

QUEAN; 1. homosexual **2.** (Scots) a young girl.

QUEEN; nine pounds.

QUEER; 1. homosexual **2.** suspect, worthless **3.** counterfeit money.

QUEER-BASHING; the beating up of homosexuals usually done by gangs often for pleasure rather than money. Also *queer-rolling*.

QUEER FELLOW; a prisoner condemned to hang.

QUEER-HAWK; (Glas) sometimes used of a homosexual but more usually a mental case.

QUEER QUARTET; the four officers detailed to watch over a man in the death cell. Two were on duty and two on call.

QUEER STREET, to be in; in financial difficulties; from a corruption of Carey Street, former home of the Bankruptcy Court, off The Strand, in London.

QUICK, on the; to obtain by stealing.

QUICKIE; sexual intercourse lasting only a short time, undertaken in a hurry often without the removal of clothing.

QUID; one pound. Originally a guinea, late 17c.

QUIFF; 1. specifically the vulva but now more generally meaning sexual intercourse **2.** a prostitute.

QUILL; folded matchbox cover used for sniffing drugs.

QUIM; as quiff (qv). A parody of the popular song 'Yes my darling daughter,' contains the lines:

> 'Mother dear, may I swim?
> Yes my darling daughter,
> Don't let the boys touch your quim
> Keep it under water'.

QUOD; old term for prison, probably first a corruption and then diminutive of quadrangle, where the prisoners exercised.

R

RAB; a till.

RABBI; (US) a senior police officer who will offer advice and protection to a younger officer and who may be able to influence his career favourably.

RABBIT; something belonging (principally) to the Navy but purloined for personal use. The origin of the word is said to be from the theft of two twists of tobacco, which were white and torpedo shaped. Two of them were stolen by a person going ashore and put in his bag but with the ends pointing out. When challenged as to what it was he replied 'My rabbit'.

RABBIT (ON), to; 1. (RS) to talk endlessly. Rabbit and pork = talk **2.** to run away.

RADICS (RADIX); (WI) the police.

RAGS; old cloths worn during menstruation.

RAINBOWS; Tuinal capsules.

RAKE, to; (Scots) to search.

RANK, to; to double cross.

RAP; (US) **1.** charge made on arrest **2.** a prison sentence.

RAP, to; to talk in West Indian dialect. Originally from the French *repartir*.

RAPSHEET; (US) charge sheet.

RASPBERRY; abusive noise made by pursing the lips together and them blowing. It comes from the rhyming slang raspberry tart = fart. A raspberry when performed correctly is meant to imitate a fart.

RAT, to; to inform to the police.

RATCATCHER; Roman Catholic.

RATTLER; 1. the underground railway (formerly a hansom cab) **2.** a woman available for free sex.

RED BAND; trusted prisoner identified by his red arm band.

RED BIDDY; cheap red wine fortified with methylated spirits. The effect on the drinker is disastrous.

RED FLAG IS UP, the; menstruation.

RED LIGHT DISTRICT; brothel quarter, so called because of the red lights hanging in windows to indicate the sexual availability of the occupants. The practice seems to have originated in Dodge City, Kansas. When train crews went to the brothels they left their red lanterns outside so they could be found easily in an emergency. This form of advertising quickly caught on.

REEFER; marijuana cigarette.

REGGIE; (pronounced with hard 'g's) a regulator or naval service policeman.

RESULT; an acquittal, usually against the odds; a lighter sentence than anticipated.

RHINO; money, dating back to the 17c. Often used for prisoner's weekly pay.

RICHARD; (RS) a good looking girl. Richard the Third = bird. Also RS for turd.

RIG, to; to make a game crooked.

RIGHT; real, as in a right liberty (qv).

RIGHT TOUCH; a lucky and unexpected acquittal.

RINGER; 1. a stolen motor vehicle with the number plates changed and either sold on or used in a robbery **2.** someone in the know who is introduced to a swindle to obtain an advantage.

RING THE BELL, to; to obtain an acquittal, usually unexpectedly. From the 'Try your strength' games at fairgrounds, where if a button was hit with sufficient force a bell rang.

RIP, to; to open a window.

RIP-OFF, to; to obtain by a swindle.

RIVER; (RS) drink. River Ouse = booze. An example of the dangers of not fully appreciating what clients are talking about and being afraid to ask comes from the solicitor preparing an alibi notice for his client and saying the man had been out boating when he had said he had 'been on the river all day.'

ROACH; butt of a marijuana cigarette, so-called because when wet it resembles a cockroach.

ROB, to ; to steal. Used with a direct object as in 'I robbed a video last week.'

ROCK; a pellet of crack.

ROCKS; 1. diamonds **2.** testicles.

ROCKS OFF, to get one's; to achieve sexual satisfaction. Often used in a derogatory sense, as in 'He gets his rocks off watching me tinkle' (qv).

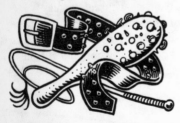

ROD; 1. a gun **2.** an overcoat.

RODGER or **ROGER, to;** to have sexual intercourse. Possibly the derivation is from the name often given to bulls. Certainly the word appears as early as 1711 in the secret diary of William Byrd of Westover where he wrote 'I rogered her lustily.' It survives today as a name for a man interested in intercourse and as a name for the penis.

ROFE; (pronounced roaf), a four-year prison sentence.

ROLL, to; to steal from a drunk.

ROLL, to be on a; to be in luck, to have a winning streak. Originally from dice but now used in sport generally, as in 'The Tigers are on a roll. They won again in Kansas tonight.'

ROLL A DRUM, to; police search of a house or flat.

ROLLER; the angry 'relative' in a badger game (qv).

ROPE; cannabis.

ROPE, the; death by hanging.

ROUND-HEELS; a boxer who is easily knocked down. The implication is that because his heels are round he falls backwards on them.

ROW-IN, to; to take a share; to go along with.

RUBBER; (US) a contraceptive, from the texture.

RUBBER CHEQUE; a cheque which is dishonoured, so-called because it bounces.

RUBBER HEEL; a detective; in England specifically one who investigates corruption in other officers.

RUBBER-HEELED MOB; the Police Complaints Bureau.

RUBE; the victim of a confidence trick, someone easily deceived.

RUMBLE; 1. a police search **2.** a fight.

RUMBLED, to be; 1. as *1.* above and **2.** to be found out.

RUMMY; a drunkard, from addiction to rum.

RUMPY PUMPY; sexual intercourse.

RUN IN IT, a; a defence in a criminal case with some chance of success.

RUNNER; 1. a small-time antique dealer **2.** bookmaker's assistant **3.** a person used to carry drugs from vendor to buyer **4.** a person given bail who absconds.

RUNNER, to do a; to escape from police or custody generally.

RUN-OUT; a mock auction.

RUN UP THE RED FLAG; to wear a sanitary towel.

RUPERT; an army officer.

RUSH ACT; a swindle in which criminals impersonate the police, a version of the corner game (qv). Usually worked on other criminals who pay bribes to the 'police' for being let off without a charge.

S

SAFE, a; a contraceptive sheath.

SALLY ANN; the Salvation Army and the rooming houses they provide for the homeless.

SALT AND PEPPER TEAM; a black and a white policeman paired to work together.

SAND; prison term for sugar.

SATCH; cotton used to strain a heroin solution before injection.

SATURDAY NIGHT SPECIAL; a cheap hand-gun produced mainly in Florida. It gets its name from its use in drunken domestic weekend quarrels.

SAUSAGE, to hide the; (Aus) to have intercourse.

SAUSAGE JOCKEY; homosexual.

SAVE IT, to; to remain a virgin thereby 'saving it' for a husband.

SCAB; a strike-breaker.

SCAM; 1. a confidence trick **2.** (US) to escape from prison.

SCARPER, to; to run away.

SCHLEP; (Yiddish) to carry, to drag around.

SCHMO(E); a fool or innocent abroad. Probably a euphemism for schmuck.

SCHMUCK; a thoroughly unpleasant person. From the Yiddish meaning penis, literally ornament.

SCHNEIDER; a Jewish person. In German *schneider* = tailor and many tailors were Jewish. Still common amongst the Cypriot community in London.

SCHOOL; euphemism for a reform school or Borstal which was more properly called college (qv) since, in its way, it was a form of higher education.

SCHOOLBOY; codeine.

SCHWARTZER; (Yiddish) a black person.

SCORCH; arson.

SCORE; 1. to obtain drugs **2.** to have sexual intercourse, as in 'Did you score last night?' From the unattractive male habit of keeping a tally of the number of women with whom they have had intercourse.

SCRAGSMAN; the hangman.

SCRAN; food, both army and prison. Originally it was the bread served in a spike.

SCREAM; an appeal against conviction or sentence.

SCREW; a prison officer.

SCREW, to; 1. to break into premises **2.** to have sexual intercourse.

SCREW AROUND, to; 1. to idle or loaf time away **2.** to have many sexual partners.

SCRIP or **SCRIPT;** a drug addict's prescription.

SCRUBBER; a girl who is reputed to be available for free sex. It can also mean a girl who is not too clean in her personal habits. Rarely used for a professional prostitute.

Originated as a description of mares in the Australian outback who mate indiscriminately.

SCRUBS, the; Wormwood Scrubs prison in West London. Although there are suggestions it is also called the *Brushes* from an allusion to scrubbing brushes and prisoners' work, the name derived from the scrubland on which the prison was built.

SEENERS; a diminutive of seen-off (qv). There is considerable use in naval slang of '-ers' eg *stoppers, gulpers*.

SEEN-OFF, to be; to be treated unfairly, given harsher punishment than merited.

SENT DOWN; sentenced to imprisonment. In the old courtrooms the cells were always under the dock and so the prisoner had to go down the steps to begin his term of imprisonment.

SET-UP; a police trap.

SHACKED UP; living in a relationship which the man, if not the woman, knows to be only temporary, eg for the duration of an army posting.

SHADE; (US) a receiver of stolen goods.

SHADES; dark glasses.

SHAG; 1. particularly strong tobacco **2.** sexual intercourse.

SHAGGED OUT; very tired, presumably from too much sexual intercourse.

SHAGGER'S BACK; (Aus) back ache of any description. How much more macho to attribute it to sexual intercourse than gardening. But, there again, think of the sexual symbolism of the old negro work song 'Digging my potatoes.'

SHAKEDOWN; 1. a search **2.** extortion. Literally the person is shaken to see what he has in his pockets **3.** a cheap night's lodgings presumably because the mattress was shaken for bugs.

SHAKES, the; trembling of the hands after an excess of alcohol or drugs.

SHAM; a policeman. There are a number of possible origins for this. One suggestion is that it is an abbreviation of shamrock, because of the number of Irishmen who were American police officers. A second is that it is short for Shamus, a detective. The third that it is an expression of the underworld's contempt for 'the finest' (qv).

SHAMEZ; (Yiddish) a policeman. In fact, technically a beadle or usher in a synagogue.

SHANK; (Army) a female.

SHANK, to; to stab. Originally to stab in the leg but now to stab anywhere. A shank itself is usually a handmade double-edged knife.

SHARK; 1. a gambler who pretends to be less than able at cards, snooker, pool, in order to induce a punter to increase the stakes after allowing the sucker to win the first few games. He then shows his true ability. **2.** a moneylender. Diminutive of loan shark (qv).

SHEBEEN; illegal drinking establishment.

SHEEP RANCH; a brothel where the girls will undertake kinky sex.

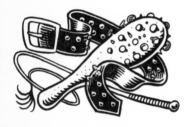

SHEEPSKIN; a certificate hung in a lawyer's office showing his qualifications.

SHEET; (US) a police record.

SHELL GAME; a variant of the three-card trick. This time the mark (qv) has to guess and bet under which of three shells a pea is hidden.

SHILL; a person who is pretending to play cards, roulette, craps etc but who is really part of the casino management. It is generally regarded by gamblers as unlucky to go to an empty table. 'Shilling' is illegal in British casinos.

SHIRTLIFTER; a homosexual.

SHIT; heroin.

SHIT, a load of; nonsense.

SHITFACED; very drunk. Probably from the necessity to kneel over the lavatory pan to vomit.

SHIT PARCEL DUTY; prison yard sweeping. So-called because prisoners throw packages of excrement into the yard from their cells at night in the absence of proper lavatory facilities.

SHIV; a knife or cut-throat razor used as a weapon. See also *chib* and *chiv*.

SHONKED, to be; to have burgled a house and found nothing worth stealing.

SHOOT UP; to inject narcotic into a vein.

SHOP, to; to inform.

SHORT EYES; child molester. Originally American but now in some use in the north of England where the word nonce (qv) is not recognised.

The derivation is possibly from the height of the victim.

SHORT HAIRS; the pubic hairs.

SHORT HAIRS, to have someone by the; to have a victim in a difficult position. From the pain suffered when the pubic hairs are pulled.

SHOUT; a round of drinks, a turn, as in 'It's my shout.' From the necessity of raising one's voice to get the barman's attention.

SHOVEL; (RS) prison. Shovel and Pick = nick.

SHOWBOAT, to; to show off, to clown around. A boxer is said to be 'showboating' when, instead of landing blows on his opponent he dances around the ring with his hands dropped, inviting the other man to try to hit him.

SHOWER; a worthless or tiresome person. Someone of no regard, as in 'You really are a shower.' Diminutive of *shower of shit*.

SHTOOK; in trouble; landed with a problem, as in 'I'm in shtook.'

SHUTEYES; (US) a sex offender, presumably because the victim tries to avoid seeing what is happening.

SHYSTER; originally a crooked lawyer, now used for crooked people or lawyers generally; a corruption of the name Eugene Scheuster, a dishonest New York lawyer of the 1850s. He so infuriated a local judge that when other lawyers misbehaved he would tell them not to indulge in 'Scheuster practices'.

SIDE, a bit on the; extra-martial relationship.

SILK; 1. (US) a rich person **2.** (WI) a white person **3.** a Queen's Counsel.

SING, to; to inform to the police or authorities.

SIPPERS; the reward for a small favour.

SIR ANTHONY; (RS) a fool. Sir Anthony Blunt = cunt. After former director of the Queen's art treasures who was a Russian spy.

SITTER; a part-time prostitute.

SIXTY-NINE; see *soixante neuf.*

SKAG; heroin.

SKATE, to; to go through a ticket barrier on the underground without paying.

SKIMMING UP; smoking cannabis.

SKIN GAME; originally any dishonest gambling game, particularly cards, but now any confidence trick. In the 18c a skin was a purse and to skin was to steal. In 19c America a skin was a shirt, and so in a swindle or rigged card game the victim was left skinned or without the shirt on his back. Skins is also a version of a four-ball golf game where a sum of money is bet on each hole and the outright winner takes the sum. If the hole is halved the money is accumulated until there is a winner of one hole.

SKINK; (UKbl) a white person; used as a term of abuse.

SKINT; (RS) without money, penniless. Boracic lint = skint.

SKIN WORKER: a thief who specialises in stealing furs.

SKIP, to; to run away without paying.

SKIPPERING; the practice of sleeping rough.

SKY; (RS) a pocket. Skyrocket = pocket.

SKYPILOT; a clergyman.

SLABBED AND SLID; dead, gone and forgotten. Prison slang for an inmate who has served his time and disappeared into the outside world.

SLAG; elderly and rather broken-down prostitute.

SLAG (OFF); to reprimand or to attack verbally.

SLAPPER; young girl of loose morals.

SLASH; the vagina.

SLASH, to have a; to urinate.

SLAUGHTER, to; to defeat heavily.

SLEEP; 1. (US) a sentence of one year **2.** (UK) a sentence of three years.

SLOP JOCKEY; an army cook.

SLOSH; 1. a coffee stall **2.** a variant of snooker where only one red ball is used, counting eight points, and a player may nominate the ball to be played instead of having to play red and then a colour. It makes for a faster, higher scoring and generally easier game.

SLOT; (Aus) gaol.

SLUNG, to be; to be acquitted.

SLUSH; counterfeit money.

SLUSH FUND; money available for bribery.

SMACK; heroin.

SMACK, to; to beat up.

SMART MONEY; money bet by those in the know who believe they have inside information that will make their gamble or investment a successful one.

SMASH; loose change or money.

SMEAR; 1. to try to destroy a reputation by making false allegations **2.** to bribe an underling.

SMOKE; opium.

SMOKE, the; London.

SMOTHER; an overcoat.

SMOTHER GAME; pickpocketing with the aid of an overcoat for cover.

SMUTTER; (Yiddish) imitation. *Smutter tom* = fake jewellery.

SNAFU; a large and frequently obvious mistake. From the acronym of 'Situation normal all fucked up'.

SNATCH; the vagina. Question: What is the difference betweeen the common cold and mononucleosis? Answer: You get a cold from snatching a kiss.

SNEEZE; an arrest.

SNIDE; 1. crooked; imitation **2.** an unpleasant remark.

SNIDE SHOOTER; imitation firearm.

SNITCH; police informer.

SNORER; (Yiddish) a beggar or scrounger.

SNOUT; 1. prison tobacco. Its origin comes from the days when smoking was forbidden in a prison and a man caught by a warder could expect to be put on punishment. A prisoner smoking would cup the cigarette in his hand and pretend to be rubbing his nose **2.** an informer.

SNOW; heroin, cocaine, morphine.

SNOWBIRD; heroin addict.

SNOWDROPPING; stealing women's underwear from clotheslines, from the time when almost all underwear was white.

SNOWDROPS; American military police, from the colour of their hats.

SNUFF MOVIE; pornographic film where at the end an actress is actually killed, often after being tortured.

SOAK; a drunkard.

SOAK, to; to obtain a quantity of money from a victim.

SOILED DOVE; euphemism for a prostitute or more commonly a girl who worked in a brothel. It was said that Etta Place, the girlfriend of Butch Cassidy and the Sundance Kid was a soiled dove from a Denver brothel.

SOIXANTE NEUF; mutual oral intercouse. From the position formed.

SOLDIER ON, to; 1. carry on and do one's best in a difficult situation **2.** (Navy) to slack.

SOUP; nitro-glycerine.

SOUPER; a watch.

SP; information. Literally, starting price. From the racing term signifying the price of a horse or dog at the beginning of a race.

SPAM; (Army) an American.

SPANKING; 1. a heavy defeat. **2.** a beating up. In either case; 'I gave him a good spanking.'

SPARE; a female available for extra-marital intercourse.

SPARE, to go; to become extremely angry.

SPARKLERS; diamonds.

SPARK OUT; unconscious, as in 'He knocked him spark out with a right hook.'

SPARROWS; dawn, very early. Contraction of *Up at sparrow's fart.*

SPEAK TO YOU; as in 'Can I speak to you?' Opening words prior to a proposal of bribery. Possibly used by a prisoner who will provide useful information to the arresting officer in exchange for bail.

SPEED; amphetamines.

SPEEDBALL; a cocaine and heroin injection.

SPIEL, to; 1. to play (from the German) **2.** to tell (tall) stories.

SPIELER; an illegal gaming joint.

SPIN; to search, as in 'We spun his drum' (qv).

SPIV; a person who dresses flashily and lives by his wits. More common in the 1940s and '50s than today. One suggestion of its origin is that it is back slang, either for 'Very important persons' (VIPs) or from police records of 'Suspected persons and itinerant vagrants'. It is possible that neither of these is correct and that the word is of Romany origin. *Spivic* was a sparrow and the word was used as one of contempt for anyone who picked up other people's leavings.

SPLIT; a detective.

SPLIT, to; 1. to sever connections **2.** to turn Queen's Evidence, to inform.

SPONDULIX; (UK) money. The term originated in the 1800s and is still current.

SPRATS, to have a handful of; vaginal stimulation. Very common in the 1950s when such a thing might be the height of sexual attainment on an evening out. Now much less common.

SPRING, to; to organise a prison escape.

SPROG; a newly enlisted soldier.

SPUNK; semen.

SQUARE-GO; (Scots) a fight without weapons.

SQUEAL, to; to inform.

SQUEALER; 1. informer **2.** (Aus) a young girl. See also *grunter*.

SQUEEZE, it's a; of something easy.

STABLE; a number of boxers, wrestlers, prostitutes etc under one management.

STAIR JUMPING; stealing from offices. Possibly from the need to escape at speed.

STALL, to; to delay.

STAR; a pimp's best prostitute.

STARDUST; cocaine.

STARKERS; naked. An abbreviation of *stark bollock naked*.

STAUNCH; police expression for a witness who it is believed will stand up to cross examination without faltering, as in 'He is staunch.'

STEAMER; 1. (RS) a fool or a mug. Steam tug = mug **2.** a horse unfancied in the early betting on whom there is suddenly a considerable amount of money laid.

STEAMING; 1. to run through a crowded train or place stealing indiscriminately **2.** (Scots) drunk.

STEP OFF, to; to die.

STICK HANDLE AROUND, to; to overcome a difficult problem; from the ice hockey term to get the puck round an opposing player.

STICKSING; (WI) pickpocketing.

STIFF; a corpse.

STIFF, to; 1. to kill **2.** to swindle.

STING; a swindle or confidence trick.

STIR; prison.

STITCH UP; to fabricate evidence.

STONES; 1. jewels **2.** testicles.

STONEY; very, as in 'stoney broke' or 'stoney rich'.

STONK, to; to hurl abuse. Originally a military term for a number of guns firing in a limited area.

STOOLIE; abbreviation of stool-pigeon (qv).

STOOL-PIGEON; semi-professional informer.

STOPPERS; to be forbidden leave, a tot of rum or conjugal relations. As in, 'The missus has put me on stoppers.'

STOREYVILLE; the brothel quarter of New Orleans. Originally jokingly named after a city alderman, Stanley Storey who promoted the ordinance which restricted prostitution to a block in the Canal Street area of the city. The name stuck.

STOTIOUS; (Scots) very drunk.

STRAIGHTEN, to; to bribe.

STRAIGHT UP; the truth, honestly obtained, as in 'These watches is straight up.'

STRAP, to; to interrogate harshly.

STREAK, to; to run naked in public. Very popular during the intervals at football and cricket matches in the 1970s.

STREET VALUE; the price of drugs paid by buyers 'on the street'.

STRETCH; a year's imprisonment.

STRIPE, to; to cut with a razor or knife.

STROKE; 1. if carried out by the speaker a successful if almost invariably dishonest piece of business **2.** if perpetrated on the speaker a thoroughly unfair piece of behaviour.

STUFFER; one who jams a telephone box and then returns to collect the money. Up to £200 a day can be made at a busy railway station.

STUMER; a cheque or banker's order. At one time these were left behind in a burglary as being worthless. A stumer therefore came to mean a mistake. Times have changed however and banker's drafts and cheques have become valuable currency for today's more sophisticated thief.

STUMER, to drop a; to make a mistake.

STUMM; (Yiddish) to remain silent, to refuse to answer questions by the police.

SUCK; 1. to commit fellatio or cunnilingus **2.** to curry favour with authority – more usually *to suck up* **3.** boring or unpleasant, as in 'This place sucks'.

SUCK HOLE; to flatter or toady. From the same stable as to brown nose (qv).

SUCK YOUR TEETH, to; to complain.

SUGAR; 1. term of endearment but often related to a man who is paying for his pleasure **2.** bribe money **3.** narcotics eg cocaine, morphine or heroin **4.** euphemism for shit, as in 'Well s . . . ugar.'

SUGAR DADDY; a man, usually elderly, who is paying for his pleasures.

SUS; the old charge under the Vagrancy Act of being a 'known and reputed thief'. Triable only before magistrates, it was very difficult to defend, consisting as it did wholly of police evidence. It fell into disfavour after the police had used it with some success against black pickpockets. Until the 1960s it was almost always used against white pickpockets

and car thieves. Civil rights groups successfully fought to have a substitute charge of 'attempted theft', which carried the right of trial by jury, introduced.

SWAG; stolen goods.

SWAGMAN; (Aus) vagabond, hiker from the swag he carries in his bundle. The swag may also be the actual bundle he carries.

SWALLOW, to; to accept defeat easily, as in a boxer who refuses to get up after a knockdown. In this usage it does not mean he has been paid to lie down, rather that he has lost heart and cannot bring himself to continue.

SWEEDEY the; derisory name given by the Metropolitan Police to regional police officers investigating corruption amongst London police during Operation Countryman. The investigation,

which generated considerable ill-feeling and produced no very clear results, was bedevilled by what the out-of-town officers saw as deliberate obstruction by the Met. The name itself refers to The Sweeney, or Flying Squad (qv).

SWEENEY; the Flying Squad. After its Irish founder, John Sweeney.

SWEET; amenable to bribery; shortened form of *sweet as a nut*.

SWEETENER; a bribe or an additional but illicit fee such as a cash payment on top of a lawyer's Legal Aid fees either to ensure that particular person's appearance in court rather than having a substitute, or in the hope it will make him perform better.

SWEETMAN; (B1) a pimp.

SWIFT, a bit; an unfair advantage, as in 'That was a bit swift.'

SWING; to hang, to be hanged.

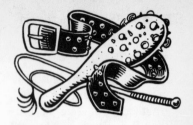

SWINGER; strictly a fashionable person in the 'swing of things', but also has a sexual connotation, meaning one who is sexually very active.

SWITCH; a massage parlour where the client gets to massage the employee.

SWITCH BLADE; American term for flick knife. The knife springs out of the handle at the press of a button.

SWITCH HITTER; a bisexual. From the baseball term for a player who can bat equally well either left or right handed.

SWOON; to take a dive, to lose a boxing or other contest deliberately.

SWORDSMAN; 1. sexually active male **2.** a receiver of stolen property.

T

T: marijuana. See also *tea*.

TAG; 1. (US) a warrant for arrest **2.** signature of writer of graffiti.

TAIL, to; to follow.

TAIL; 1. sexual intercourse **2.** the vagina **3.** a prostitute.

TAILED OFF; horse which has lost contact with others in a race. It can no longer see the other horses' tails.

TAKE; share of proceeds.

TAKE, on the; police officer susceptible to bribery.

TAKE FOR A RIDE, to; 1. to take to a lonely spot and execute **2.** to swindle.

TALLY, the; (Scots) a corner shop. To an older generation these were always seemingly run by Italians whereas now they are run by Asians.

TANK; a prison cell.

TANK, to go in the; to lose a boxing contest deliberately, usually for betting purposes. See also *take a dive*.

TAPE, to; to size up.

TAPPER; a beggar.

TEA; marijuana.

TEALEAF; (RS) thief. Tealeaf = thief.

TEAM; gang.

TEASER; also known as cock teaser. A woman who indicates her availability for sexual intercourse but then refuses after stimulating the male. In horse breeding terminology the teaser is a worthless stallion who sexually excites the mare and ensures she is in season when the star of the show is led out to cover her. Occasionally the teaser gets carried away before the stud grooms can prevent an unintended coupling, which can have disastrous financial results.

TECATA; heroin.

TECHNICOLOUR YAWN; (Aus) vomit.

TECRAM; (back slang) market.

TELEPHONE NUMBERS; an excessively high price such as wanted by a barrister to defend an accused or a manager for his boxer's appearance. As in 'He's talking telephone numbers.'

TENDERLOIN; (US) literally a particularly succulent cut of steak but now a city district where there is the greatest opportunity for graft and corruption. It stems from the old New York City 29th precinct, which policed an area from 23rd to 42nd Street and which includes Times Square, the notable hangout for all sorts of unsavoury offerings.

THATCHERVILLES; the cardboard cities of tramps which have grown up in areas of London such as Lincoln's Inn Fields and Waterloo. The word has a similar meaning to *Hoovervilles*, the hobo jungles of the American depression, and the French *Bidonvilles*, iron shanty towns.

THREE-CARD MONTE; American name for *find the lady* (qv) given respectability in that monte is a Mexican gambling game.

THREE-CARD TRICK; sleight of hand trick in which the mug punter is led to believe he can spot which of three cards is the queen. Also known as *find the lady* (qv), *three-card monte* (qv). See also *keep dog*.

THROW; to lose a contest deliberately, usually for betting purposes. One of the best known instances in sport of a game being thrown was in the Baseball World Series of 1919 when the Chicago White Sox deliberately lost the World Series. They became known, for a time, as the Chicago Black Sox.

TICKLE; 1. money obtained in a slightly *louche* way eg a successful theft, con trick, win on the horses **2.** an unexpected arrest (from the police point of view).

TICKLERS; contraceptives with small rubber studs designed to enhance vaginal stimulation.

TIDDLY; 1. inebriated **2.** (Navy) smartly dressed.

TIE ONE ON; to get very drunk.

TIME; prison sentence. One chairman of quarter sessions told a man who had stolen a clock 'If it's time you want I'll give you three months.'

TIME, have you got the?; old enquiry of punters to street prostitutes. The traditional reply was 'Yes, if you've got the money.'

TINKLE; to urinate.

TIP OFF; warning of impending disaster such as a police raid.

TITHEAD; a policeman (from the shape of the helmet). A common chant at football matches.

TOBY; Police division. See also *manor*.

TOD, to be on one's; (CRS) to be alone. Tod Sloan = alone. Tod Sloan was an American jockey who rode in England in the early 1900s who was so successful that he was usually out in front – alone.

TOE-RAG; hopeless person. From the bandages beggars used to wear on their feet.

TOMATO CAN; (US) a boxer with no chance of winning; on the bill merely to make up the numbers.

TOM; 1. a prostitute **2.** (RS) jewellery = tomfoolery.

TOM AND DICK; (RS) sick as in vomiting. It can also mean a more serious illness.

TOM SQUAD; the Vice Squad.

TOM TIT; (RS) to defecate. Tom tit = shit.

TON; 1. £100 **2.** 100 mph. and therefore in the '50s and '60s a Ton-up Boy, was a driver or motorcyclist whose machine could achieve the speed.

TONGUE PIE; cunnilingus.

TOOL; 1. a weapon or house-breaking implement **2.** the penis.

TOOLED-UP; carrying weapons.

TOOT, on the; out on the town, having a good time.

TOOT A LINE; sniff cocaine.

TOPPED, to be; to be hanged.

TOPPED (HIM or HERSELF), gone and; to have committed suicide. When a member of EXIT, an organisation promoting euthanasia appeared charged with manslaughter there was a demonstration of support by his – mainly elderly – supporters.

One regular attender at the court asked his colleague who these people in woolly hats and carrying balloons were. He was told they were supporters of euthanasia and asked what that was. 'Old-dear topping,' was the reply.

TORCH; a person who commits arson, generally for insurance purposes.

TORCH, to carry a; unrequited love, often of a prostitute for her pimp.

TORPEDO A DRUM, to; to carry out a house-breaking.

TOSHER; a Roman Catholic. From the Protestant belief that some aspects of the teachings of the Roman Catholic church are tosh.

TOSSER; a fool or worthless person. Someone who has masturbated so much he has ruined his brain.

TOSS OFF; to masturbate.

TOTTER; 1. a rag and bone man **2.** a person whose driving licence has 12 or more penalty points against it when all the endorsements are added together or totted up and so becomes liable for a period of disqualification.

TOTTIE; a girl available for sexual intercourse.

TOUCH; 1. money successfully and slightly dishonestly obtained by a gamble or by borrowing; **2.** an unexpected acquittal on a criminal charge.

TOUCHING THE DOG'S ARSE; taking and driving away a motor vehicle. South London expression from the initial letters of 'taking and driving away'.

TOUCH OF THE SECONDS; a change of mind (second thoughts) often about embarking on a criminal or foolhardy exercise.

TOUGH TITTY; hard luck.

TOYBOY; the younger lover of an older woman.

TRAMP'S LAGGING; three months imprisonment. Considered severe since tramps would normally have received a sentence of a week or two at the worst.

TRAPS; (Aus) police.

TRICK; the act performed by a prostitute and thereby her client.

TROD; stolen goods, as in 'I didn't know it was trod.' Probably from 'Trodden on and bent.' The word was originally of West Indian usage but is now more general in the south of England.

TROTS; 1. (US) harness racing or trotting **2.** (UK) diarrhoea. In America and Canada where harness race meetings are often held in the evening such meets were described as night trots. This, of course, has a completely different meaning in the United Kingdom.

TRUE BILL; (US) a correct allegation; from the Bill handed down by the Grand Jury to determine whether a defendant should stand his trial. With the growth of the magistracy which held committal proceedings to determine the same thing the Grand Jury eventually became obsolete, though it is still to be found in a number of American States.

TRUSTY; a prisoner trusted by the authorities and therefore allowed certain freedom within and sometimes outside the prison.

TUKEY BOY; (UKbl) a gullible youth.

TUMBLE; a drink.

TUMBLE, to; 1. to understand **2.** to have sexual intercourse.

TUMBLED, to be; to be found out or arrested.

TURF; territory occupied by a criminal gang and one which will be defended against intruders.

TURN IN, to; to inform on.

TURN OVER, to; to search.

TURQUOISE; a girl who will permit anal intercourse. A contraction of 'Turk ways' derived from the alleged enthusiasm of Turkish men for that form of intercourse.

TURTLES; (RS) turtle doves = gloves.

TWAT; 1. the vagina. Despite this usage of the word since the 17th century, the poet Robert Browning used the word to mean clothing, describing it as part of a nun's attire **2.** a fool.

TWEEDLE, on the, or **TWEEDLING; 1.** stealing jewellery by substituting worthless items **2.** passing off inferior goods by pretending they are well-known lines. (Particularly common in the sale of cheap perfume.)

TWIRL; skeleton key.

TWO AND EIGHT; (RS) nervous. Two and eight = state.

TWO-BACKED BEAST; the act of sexual intercourse.

TWO-TIME LOSER; (UK) an accused with previous convictions. In some American States the penalties for a conviction depend upon whether the defendant has a conviction for that offence before. It is possible to plea bargain with the prosecution so that in return for a plea of guilty to an offence they will not ask for what might amount to a double penalty because of the prior conviction.

TWO'D UP; number of prisoners in a cell. Can also be '*three'd up*' etc.

TWO'S UP; to share, as in 'Two's up on your fag?'

TWO-UP; illegal Australian gambling game where each player tosses a coin in the air and bets on how it will land.

U

UMBRELLA BRIGADE; the Special Branch (from their style of dress).

UNCLE; a receiver of stolen goods, sometimes a pawnbroker, the two professions often working hand-in-hand.

UNCLE JOHN; (Scots) a pawnbroker.

UNDER THE TONGUE; the common method of passing drugs to a prisoner by a visiting wife or girlfriend when kissing their loved one goodbye.

UNDER WRAPS; a horse ridden to give less than his best in expectation of a betting coup next time out.

UP AND DOWNER; railway police term for an adult and a juvenile arrested together. One must go to the adult and the other to the juvenile court.

UPCHUCK; to vomit.

UP FRONT; money paid to a solicitor on account of fees in a criminal defence case.

UPHILL GARDENING; anal intercourse.

UPPERS, on his; to be broke, down and out; ie the soles of his shoes had worn away and all that was left was the upper part.

UPPERS AND DOWNERS; amphetamines and barbiturates, ie stimulants and depressives.

UP SHIT CREEK WITHOUT A PADDLE; out of luck, in a hopeless situation. The abbreviated version *up the creek* is now in common usage but originally it derived from homosexual argot meaning being caught in the act of sodomy.

UP THE RIVER, to be sent; (US) to be sent to Ossining (Sing Sing) prison on the Hudson River.

UP THE STEPS; to be committed for sentence (or trial) at the crown court. From the fact that the dock in a courtroom at assizes or quarter sessions had to be entered by going up a flight of steps.

UP YOURS; a shortened version of *stick it up your arse* implying disbelief or rejection.

URGER; a con-man's associate, particularly in the three-card trick.

U.S. DAY; old prison term for the day when fish was served, usually a Friday. The US stands for unconditional surrender (of the fish!).

USER; a taker of drugs.

U.S.I.; unlawful sexual intercourse with a girl under the age of 16.

V

VAG; short form of vagrant.

VAG CHARGE; a charge under the Vagrancy Act used for dealing with petty offences such as begging, loitering with intent to steal.

VAMPIRE; an extortionist.

VATICAN ROULETTE; birth control method using the so-called 'safe' part of the menstrual cycle the only one which does not offend against Roman Catholic teaching.

VEGETARIAN; a prostitute who will not perform fellatio on a client; not a meat eater (qv).

VELVET; 1. illicitly obtained money **2.** money available for free-spending for example on a holiday.

VERBAL(S); a remark alleged by the police to have been made by a suspect either wholly or in part admitting the offence. This has been a constant source of aggravation in criminal trials and is one which, with better recording of interviews, eg on tape and video, may well die out.

Strictly speaking, from the defendant's point of view the 'verbal' is implicitly false.

VIC; a victim either of a mugging or a con trick; a sucker.

VIG; short for vigorish **1.** interest on a loan shark's nut (qv), generally 20 per cent per week. It is said that a clever loan shark can keep a victim paying off the vig without ever getting to clear or even reduce the principle sum loaned. **2.** the percentage earned by a gambling house **3.** vigilante. By no means common in the United Kingdom but likely to be of wider use if the Guardian Angels are eventually allowed to police the underground system.

VILLAIN; police term for local hooligan; the implication is that

he is a hard man with whom to deal or meet in a fight.

VILLE, the; Pentonville prison in the Caledonian Road, London, which now houses short-term prisoners.

VIPER MAD; (Can) addicted to marijuana.

VISITING FIREMAN; a free-spending visitor from out of town. The term is used by the police etc who have to entertain a member of another force sent to conduct part of an investigation or collect a prisoner. It is also used of conference delegates. Often they will have been provided with the addresses of women who are likely to provide sexual favours in return for a night on the town.

VOLUNTEER; a young male prostitute.

WAD; 1. money, **2.** chewing tobacco.

WAG; the penis, especially a small boy's.

WAGON; 1. the police van or Black Maria **2.** see *waterwaggon*.

WALK THE BRICKS, to; (USpol) to patrol on foot.

WALL-EYED; very drunk; the inebriated state of resembling a person with a severe cast in one eye.

WALLFLOWER; a prisoner who talks of nothing but escape or life outside prison.

WANK, to; to masturbate.

WANKER; person of no account, a fool.

WASH, at the; theft from a man whilst he washes at a public convenience. Derives from the time when men would take off their jackets in a public washroom to have a proper wash. Although this form of theft is no longer common a more sophisticated version has been seen recently. A team of criminals were recently sentenced for going into golf-club locker rooms removing credit cards and cheque books, using them and then returning them in the three hours it takes for a round to be played. It is also common to find petty thefts from football and rugby club changing rooms, another modern version of 'at the wash'.

WASTE, to; 1. to kill **2.** to destroy or mutilate.

WATERWAGON, to be on the; to be teetotal or more usually not to be touching alcohol for a period following a heavy bout of drinking.

WAVE, to; to bend a playing card for the purposes of identification.

WAY DOWN SOUTH IN DIXIE; fellatio.

WEAKHEART; (WI) the police.

WEAK SISTER; police informer, untrusted member of a gang, not necessarily female.

WEDGE; a bundle of money.

WEED; tobacco generally and now specifically cannabis.

WEED, to; 1. to spend part of the proceeds of a theft; to take more than a rightful share of the money **2.** to steal from an employer **3.** to steal from a place where a crime has already been committed. A defence in criminal cases is that a burglary has already taken place and the accused merely went into the shop to see what had happened. Even if the defence fails there is still the opportunity of a variant of the story in mitigation that the accused was not the original perpetrator.

WEEKEND; a very short period of imprisonment.

WEIGH-OFF, to; to sentence (especially to prison).

WELCHER; see *welsher*.

WELL; very, as in 'well drunk'.

WELL HUNG; having large genitalia.

WELLY, to; (Liverpool) to kick.

WELSHER; a thief or cheat, a bookmaker who does not pay his debts, from the generalisation that the Welsh were dishonest, as in

> Taffy was a Welshman, Taffy was a thief.
> Taffy came to my house and stole a piece of beef.

WET SEASON; (Aus) menstruation.

WHACK; a share, usually of money but also of sex in the abstract, as in 'Are you getting your fair whack?'

WHACK, to; to beat up, as in 'I gave him a bit of a whack.'

WHACK OFF; to masturbate.

WHAM BAM THANK YOU MA'AM; quick, uninvolved sexual intercourse often with a stranger. Another version of the phrase is *Whip it in, whip it out and wipe it.*

WHEELER DEALER; someone who buys and sells or

puts together deals which are often on the borderline of honesty.

WHEELMAN; an expert driver, a getaway driver. A necessity on a team of armed robbers, but one who is likely to receive a shorter sentence than the people who actually went across the pavement.

WHEELS; a motor vehicle, particularly a stolen one to be used in a robbery.

WHIP; 1. (US) police sergeant **2.** a collection. Short for *whipround*.

WHIP, to; to steal by snatching.

WHIPPET; shotgun with two-thirds of the barrel sawn off.

WHISPER, to; to inform.

WHISTLE, to blow the; to inform.

WHITE GIRL; cocaine.

WHITE LADY; heroin.

WHITE NURSE; morphine.

WHITEWASH; the cover-up of police, political or other corruption or misconduct by the holding of an enquiry which absolves those under investigation from blame.

WHITEY; (Bl) white people in general, used as a term of abuse.

WHIZZ, to; to pickpocket.

WHO DUNNIT ?; meat pies served in prison. 'Who killed the prison cat? It's who dunnit for dinner.'

WICK, to get on one's; to get on one's nerve. Literally penis. Hampton Wick = prick.

WICKED; successful, enjoyable, as in 'It was a wicked film.' Now mostly used as West Indian or teenage slang, it can be traced back to the 1920s.

WIENIE; the penis, so called from its resemblance to a Vienna sausage.

WIENIE WIGGLER; an indecent exposer.

WILLIE TWEAKER; a practical joke.

WIND AND PISS, to be full of; to be a boaster or bragger. There are a number of such phrases of which this is the most common. Another is *full of shit and sticks*.

WINDJAMMER; (Aus) male homosexual.

WINGER; 1. a colleague, friend **2.** a magistrate, usually experienced, who sits on the right of the chairman of a bench of lay justices and who is consulted more than the third member over questions of bail, guilt and sentencing.

WINGY; (US) a one-armed man. (The one-armed Dixieland trumpeter was known as 'Wingy' Manone.)

WIRE; 1. information, from the use of ticker-tape machines, 'What's the wire (say)?' **2.** a pickpocket **3.** a signal used between card cheats. 'I sent him a wire.'

WIRED UP, to be; to be on drugs.

WIRE TO WIRE; (US) from start to finish, used particularly of a horse which leads from start to finish of a race.

WITH THE CORNER UP; disbelief.

WOG; any non-white, supposedly from the euphemism 'wily (or worthy) oriental gentleman'.

WOG-BOX; large and portable stereo.

WOOD, Charlie or Mr; a police truncheon. 'If you don't come quiet I'll introduce you to my friend Charlie.'

WOODEN KIMONO; a coffin.

WOODENTOP; 1. a uniformed police officer **2.** a lay magistrate **3.** a guardsman. From the belief that none are particularly bright.

WOOLLY; a uniformed policeman.

WOOLLYBACK; (Liverpool) a hick, anyone not from Liverpool.

WORK; 1. criminal behaviour generally. **2.** crooked cards.

WORK A FLANKER; to obtain by stealth or a trick.

WORK A GINGER, to; (Aus) to rob a prostitute's client.

WORK FROM A BOOK, to; to run call girls as opposed to street prostitutes.

WORKING GIRL; a prostitute.

WRINKLY; someone older than the speaker (usually anyone over 40).

X

X; ten dollars.

XX; twenty dollars.

Y

YAHOO; a vicious person, from *Gulliver's Travels.*

YANCING; (Yiddish) sexual intercourse.

YAP; 1. a fool or dupe **2.** a farmer **3.** a petty swindler.

YAP, to; to talk or tell a tale.

YARD; (WI) **1.** home **2.** a flat or house **3.** Jamaica **4.** 100. Although when used it usually refers to money it is also used by tickets touts who are left with more than they can sell, as in 'Anyone want a ticket? I've got a yard left.' **5.** (US) originally

1000, now usually devalued to 100 – again used principally in monetary terms **6.** Scotland Yard.

YARD, on the; to be in prison.

YARDBIRD; prisoner.

YARDIE; (WI) a member of a criminal gang of that name.

YEAR; a dollar bill.

YEGG or **YEGGMAN;** a safebreaker said to be after John Yegg the first safeblower to use nitro-glycerine; other versions of its origin are that the word was used for a professional killer employed by Chinese Tongs or that it comes from the German *jaeger* = hunter. Another suggestion is that a yegg was a travelling burglar moving from city to city, and yet another that it meant a beggar. (Although the word is American dating only from about 1880 it was used by

Conan Doyle in *Sherlock Holmes*.

YELLOW; to be lacking in spirit, cowardly.

YELLOW PERIL; prison term for vegetable soup.

YELLOW STUFF; gold coins, usually counterfeit.

YENTZER; (Yiddish) a racketeer, originally a cheat.

YOB; (back slang) boy; an unpleasant uncouth youth.

YOCKELE; (Yiddish) a non-Jewish person.

YODEL, to; to perform cunnilingus.

Z

ZAFTIG; (Yiddish) an attractive woman from the literal meaning 'juicy'.

ZAP, to; to kill, often with a burst of machine gun fire.

ZEN; LSD.

ZIFF; a juvenile thief.

ZILCH; nothing.

ZING, to; to bet heavily, particularly at dice.

ZIT; a pimple, sometimes a love bite.

ZOMBIE; 1. a drug taker **2.** a gambler who shows no emotion, win or lose **3.** a horse which shows no pep in running **3.** a policewoman **4.** a particularly disagreeable prison officer, one more dead than alive.

ZOO; a prison. From the prison in Kalamazoo.

ZOOK; a prostitute.

BIBLIOGRAPHY

CHAPMAN, Robert L.; (1987) *American Slang,* New York, Harper & Row.

DE SOLA, Ralph; (1988) *Crime Dictionary*, New York, Facts on File Publications.

FABIAN, Robert; (1970) *The Anatomy of Crime*, London, Pelham Books.

FABIAN, Robert; (1955) *Fabian of the Yard*, London, Heirloom Modern World Library.

GREEN, Jonathon; (1984) *The Dictionary of Contemporary Slang*, London, Pan Books.

GREEN, Jonathon; (1984) *Newsspeak*, London, Routledge & Keegan Paul.

GREEN, Jonathon (1988) *The Slang Thesaurus*, Harmondsworth, Penguin Books.

MAURER, David W.; (1981) *Language of the Underworld*, Kentucky, The University of Kentucky Press.

MCDONALD, James; (1988) *A Dictionary of Obscenity, Taboo and Euphemism*, London, Sphere Books.

PARTRIDGE, Eric; (1961) *A Dictionary of the Underworld*, London, Routledge & Keegan Paul.

PARTRIDGE, Eric (1986) *The Penguin Dictionary of Historical Slang*, Harmondsworth, Penguin.

PATRICK, James; (1973) *A Glasgow Gang Observed*, London, Eyre Methuen.

SCARNE, John; (1961) *Scarne's Complete Guide to Gambling*, New York, Simon & Schuster.

SIFAKIS, Carl; (1982) *The Encyclopaedia of American Crime*, New York, Facts on File Publications.

STROUD, Carsten; (1988) *Close Pursuit*, Markham, Ontario, Penguin Books.

TEMPEST, Paul; (1950) *Lag's Lexicon*, London, Routledge & Keegan Paul.

WENTWORTH, Harold, and Flexner, S. B.; (1960) *Dictionary of American Slang*, London, George G. Harrap & Co Ltd.